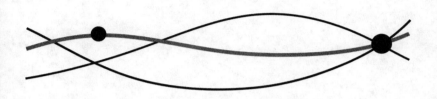

ACTS

PRINCIPLES OF VICTORY
AND PERSEVERANCE

Acts

Principles of Victory and Perseverance

F. Wayne Mac Leod

Authentic
MEDIA

00 09 08 07 06 05 04   7 6 5 4 3 2 1
Published by Authentic Media
129 Mobilization Drive, Waynesboro, GA 30830 USA   authenticusa@stl.org
and 9 Holdom Avenue, Bletchley, Milton Keynes, Bucks, MK1 1QR, UK

ISBN: 1-932805-01-X

Cover design: Paul Lewis

Contents

Preface

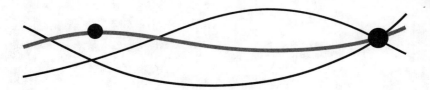

As I have worked though the Acts of the Apostles over the last few months, I have become aware of many themes flowing through the book. One of those themes is the clash between the kingdom of God and the kingdom of Satan. From the opening chapter to the end of the book, there appears to be a great spiritual battle raging. Satan is doing his utmost to destroy the work the Spirit of God has begun. You will discover through it all, however, the power of a great and sovereign God who can use even human sin and the tactics of the devil to accomplish his great overall purposes.

This book is an attempt to open up the Acts of the Apostles to the average reader. I would encourage you to take your time working through it. Use this commentary as a devotional guide for your times with the Lord. You may also want to use it as a study guide for a larger group. Each chapter concludes with some questions for consideration and some suggestions for prayer. Take time to think and pray about these matters. Be sure to read the Bible passage quoted for each chapter. Remember that this book is only a guide. I trust that it will also be a blessing. May God bless you as you read.

1

The Promise of the Spirit

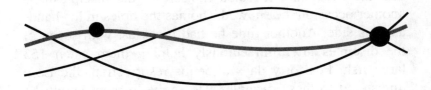

Read Acts 1:1–11

I t is generally agreed that Luke, the author of the Gospel of Luke, is also the author of the Acts of the Apostles. Luke addressed both these writings to Theophilus. Some people believe that Theophilus was an actual person living in the days of the apostles. The name "Theophilus" comes from two Greek words: *theos* meaning "God" and *philos* meaning "love." By combining these two Greek words, we get the meaning "lover of God." This has led some to conclude that Luke was writing to all lovers of God and not to a specific individual.

Luke mentioned in verse 1 that he had written another book in which he wrote about what Jesus did and taught until he was taken up into heaven. The book he was referring to was the Gospel of Luke. In Acts, his second book, Luke would tell the story of how the early church took the message of Jesus Christ into the world.

Luke began this second book with the certainty of the

resurrection of Christ (verse 3). This formed the basis for his book. Had Jesus not risen, there would never have been a book of Acts. Jesus had shown himself to the apostles and proven to them by many convincing signs that he was alive. How had the Lord done this? There was the sign of the empty tomb. When the apostles had gone to the tomb, the body of our Lord was no longer there. He had risen. He appeared to them while they were in the upper room after his death. Though the doors were locked, Jesus came into the room and revealed himself to the disciples. On another occasion, he showed Thomas the holes in his hands and his side. Another time he had breakfast with seven of the disciples after miraculously helping them catch 153 large fish. For forty days after his resurrection, the Lord ministered to these disciples. He spoke to them about the kingdom of God. There was no doubt at all in the minds of these disciples that this Jesus, who was crucified, was also raised from the dead.

Having assured us of the reality of the resurrection, Luke now tells us about the promise of the Holy Spirit. Someone has said that this book could rightly be called the book of the Acts of the Holy Spirit. We have already said that this book could never have been written if it were not for the resurrection of our Lord. Neither could this book have been written if it were not for the ministry of the Holy Spirit in the lives of the apostles. We need to examine what Luke tells us here about the Holy Spirit.

When Jesus appeared to his disciples after his resurrection, he told them not to leave the city of Jerusalem until they had received the promised Holy Spirit (verse 4). Why did Jesus give this command to his disciples? While we are not particularly told, it is obvious that the disciples, at this point, did not have a full understanding of the work of Christ. They were also without power as witnesses of the gospel. Without the ministry of the Holy Spirit in their lives, these men would have done more harm than good to the cause of Christ.

It is important to note here that these disciples had three years of personal training with the Lord himself. No seminary could have given them this experience and preparation for ministry. Simply to see him perform his miracles would have been life changing. They had seen the resurrected Jesus. They knew the truth of Jesus. If ever there was a group of men ready to move out into evangelism, humanly speaking, it was these men. However, Jesus told them to stay home. Without the ministry and the power of the Spirit of God, they were destined to fail. There is an important lesson for us here.

This talk about the coming of the Holy Spirit seemed to spark an interest in the minds of the disciples. They asked Jesus if it was at this point that he would restore the kingdom to Israel (verse 6). Ever since the people of God had been taken into captivity by the Assyrians and Babylonians, they had been under foreign domination. Israel had been ruled by the Assyrians and Babylonians, the Persians, the Greeks, and now the Romans. The Jews longed for the day when they would be set free from foreign domination. They resented foreigners telling them what they could and could not do in their own country. When Jesus spoke to his disciples about the coming of the Holy Spirit, there was hope that this Spirit would reestablish an independent nation of Israel. Their understanding of the coming ministry of the Holy Spirit was confused.

Jesus clarified for the disciples what the ministry of the Holy Spirit would be. He told them that when the Holy Spirit came on them, they would be his witnesses in Jerusalem, Judea, Samaria, and the ends of the earth (verse 8). This is an important verse in relation to the ministry of the Holy Spirit. The ministry of the Holy Spirit is to empower believers in presenting Christ to the world. This is what Jesus had told his disciples earlier: "When the Counselor comes, whom I will send to you from the Father, the Spirit of truth who goes out from the Father, he will testify about me. And you also must testify, for you have been with me from the beginning" (John 15:26–27). It is the desire of the Holy Spirit to point men and women to the Lord Jesus. All that the Spirit does has this as its objective. When the Holy Spirit ministers through us, it is so that the Lord Jesus will be glorified and clearly presented to the world. This is what would take place in the lives of the disciples when the Holy Spirit came on them.

Do you want to know if the Spirit of God is in a particular ministry? Do you want to know if the Spirit of God is working in your life? The test is to be found in Acts 1:8. Any ministry of the Holy Spirit will point men and women to the Lord Jesus. A Spirit-filled life is a life that is focused on Christ.

Having said these things, the Lord Jesus was then taken up to heaven in the sight of the disciples. He went up in a cloud. As the disciples looked up in awe, two angels reminded them that the day was coming when the Lord Jesus would return in the same manner as he left (verse 11). Matthew 24:30 tells us: "At that time the sign of the Son of Man will appear in the sky, and all the nations of the earth will mourn. They will see the Son of Man coming on the clouds of the sky, with power and great glory."

The apostle John also tells us that the Lord will return in the clouds: "Look, he is coming with the clouds, and every eye will see him, even those who pierced him; and all the peoples of the earth will mourn because of him. So shall it be! Amen" (Revelation 1:7).

Jesus left in a cloud, and he will one day return in a cloud. What a day that will be! We will see him face to face. Meanwhile, there is much work to be done. The Bible tells us that not everyone will be happy to see the return of the Lord Jesus. For those who have rejected him, this day will be a horrible day. It was for this reason that the Holy Spirit was given. He will use us to point men and women to the Savior. He will use us to prepare men and women to face the day when we all will stand before the Lord and give an account of our lives. There are many souls to be won before that day. The Lord Jesus challenged his disciples to step out in the power of the Holy Spirit and be his witnesses. That challenge is for us as well.

For Consideration:

- Why is it so important that we understand the ministry of the Holy Spirit?

- What is the difference between a ministry motivated by human strength and wisdom and one motivated and empowered by the Holy Spirit?

- This passage leads us to believe that the work of the Holy Spirit was essential if the apostles were going to accomplish anything for the Lord. Does this apply to us today as well?

- How can you tell if your ministry is one that is led and empowered by the Holy Spirit?

For Prayer:

- Ask the Lord to help you to be more sensitive to the work and leading of the Holy Spirit in your life.

- Ask him to forgive you for the times you believed that you could serve him in your own strength and wisdom.

- Thank the Lord that you know him as your Savior. Thank him for the ministry of the Spirit of God that revealed the Lord Jesus to you.

- Take a moment to pray that the Lord would use you to be his witness in a very particular way.

2
Preparation for the Spirit

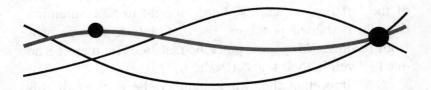

Read Acts 1:12–26

One of the last commands of our Lord to his disciples was that they remain in Jerusalem until they had received the promised Holy Spirit. The disciples, no doubt, had many questions about this coming event. How would they know that the Holy Spirit had come to them? When would these things take place? The Lord had not given them answers to these questions. All he had told them was that it would happen in Jerusalem and that they were to wait in that city until the promise was fulfilled. It was in obedience to these instructions that the disciples returned to Jerusalem after the ascension of the Lord on the Mount of Olives.

Notice here how they passed their time as they waited for the Holy Spirit. Verse 14 tells us that they joined together constantly in prayer with the women and the brothers of Jesus. The history of revival shows us that the coming of the Spirit of God in power is associated with the fervent prayer of

God's people. There was no exception here. Before pouring out his Spirit on his people, God moved them to prayer. We are not told what they prayed. We can be assured, however, that their prayers were prayers of confession and seeking the direction of the Lord.

Notice also that these disciples not only committed themselves to prayer but to the reading and meditation of the Word of God (verses 15–16). They needed direction and encouragement at this point in their lives. As they prayed and sought to make sense of what had happened over the course of the last few weeks, the Lord brought to their attention two Old Testament passages. The first of these passages was from Psalms: "May their place be deserted; let there be no one to dwell in their tents" (Psalm 69:25).

It is important that we remember the context of this chapter in Acts. The Lord Jesus had just been crucified. The disciples could not help but see the injustice of this crucifixion. They also knew that if their Lord was crucified, they too were in danger. Never very far from their minds was the recent betrayal of Judas. That betrayal was like a dagger in their hearts. In their distress, they were reminded of Psalm 69. These New Testament believers in their present circumstances could personally identify with the Psalmist. Psalm 69 spoke directly to them. Luke only quotes part of the Psalm. We need to look at the greater context of verse 25 in this Psalm.

> Save me, O God, for the waters have come up to my neck. . . . Those who hate me without reason outnumber the hairs of my head; many are my enemies without cause, those who seek to destroy me. I am forced to restore what I did not steal. . . . For I endure scorn for your sake, and shame covers my face. I am a stranger to my brothers, an alien to my own

mother's sons; . . . Those who sit at the gate mock me, and I am the song of the drunkards. . . . You know how I am scorned, disgraced and shamed; all my enemies are before you. Scorn has broken my heart and has left me helpless; I looked for sympathy, but there was none, for comforters, but I found none. They put gall in my food and gave me vinegar for my thirst. . . . Pour out your wrath on them; let your fierce anger overtake them. May their place be deserted; let there be no one to dwell in their tents.
(Psalm 69:1, 4, 7–8, 12, 19–21, 24–25)

It is easy to see how this verse related to the disciples. Like the Psalmist, the disciples of Jesus had many enemies. Sometimes these enemies were the members of their own family (as in the case of Judas). People were mocking them and their faith. You can almost hear their enemies asking what would become of their faith now that their Lord had been crucified. As the disciples meditated on this Psalm, their attention would have been drawn to verse 21. Here the Psalmist mentioned that they gave him vinegar to drink. The disciples would have seen a reference to the Lord Jesus and how the soldiers had given him vinegar to drink while he was on the cross. Of particular interest to them also would have been verse 25 where the Psalmist spoke about the tent of his enemy being empty. All the disciples had to do was to look around them in the room and see that Judas's place at the table was deserted. As the disciples meditated on this passage of Scripture, they were no doubt encouraged. Their God was in control. The events of the past several weeks had been predicted long ago.

The second passage the Lord gave the disciples at this time was from another Psalm: "May his days be few; may another take his place of leadership" (Psalm 109:8). As they meditated on this verse, the Lord spoke to them about Judas. His days had been few. They had been cut short by a tragic suicide. Of particular importance was the second half of this verse that said: "May another take his place of leadership." By means of this passage of Scripture, the Lord revealed to his disciples that they were to find another person to replace Judas.

As these early believers waited for the outpouring of the Holy Spirit, they committed themselves to seeking God through the study of his Word. Through the Word, the Lord gave them encouragement in their pain and direction in their confusion. Having sensed the direction of the Lord, Peter stood up and challenged these believers to obey what the Lord was telling them. Plans were immediately made to find a successor to Judas. When God spoke, they listened. In preparation for the coming of the Spirit of God, the early church committed to absolute and immediate obedience to the revealed will of God.

How often has God spoken to us through his Word? We hear his voice and make a mental note that we will someday have to do something about it. Meanwhile, Satan succeeds in getting us to put off our obedience to a later day. The Spirit of God is grieved by our disobedience.

There were certain qualifications necessary for the individual who would replace Judas (verses 21–22). The candidate had to be an eyewitness of the baptism, resurrection, and ascension of Christ. He also had to have been with the disciples the entire time the Lord ministered among them. This individual, in other words, had to have had a personal experience with the Lord Jesus. A second-hand knowledge of the Lord Jesus was not sufficient. Should this not be a requirement for every church leader in our day as well? While none of us can claim to have physically seen the Lord, is it not logical to require that every church leader have the experience of knowing the Lord Jesus personally in his heart? The apostles refused to allow anyone to become a candidate for the position of apostle who did not have a first-hand experience with the Lord Jesus.

Notice how these believers chose the replacement for Judas. First, they looked among themselves for those who were qualified for the ministry. They found two such men. Second, they recognized that because the ultimate decision belonged to the Lord, they made this a subject of prayer. They asked the Lord to choose for them. Believing in a sovereign God, they cast lots (verse 26). They did not leave this matter to chance. Prayer preceded the casting of lots. It was their sincere belief that the Lord himself had a particular man in mind to replace Judas. They removed themselves from the ultimate decision. Their own preferences were not important. This was not a popularity contest. The Lord himself would decide. They were willing to accept his decision, whatever it might be.

How often do we get caught up in our own ideas and preferences? Are we willing to let the Lord decide what to do with our lives? As these early believers waited for the outpouring of the Spirit, they were willing to die to their own ideas so that the will of the Lord could be done. They expected God to answer their prayer and show them the person he had chosen to replace Judas. They expected the lot to fall on the man of God's choosing. When the lot fell on Matthias, it was with confidence in the choice of God that the apostles welcomed him into the ministry of apostle.

What does all of this have to do with us today? In preparation for the coming of the Holy Spirit, the early church committed to prayer, meditation, and immediate obedience to the revealed will of God. In choosing a successor for Judas, these believers expected God to reveal his will to them. They chose to let him decide and put aside their own personal preferences. It is in this context that the Spirit of God fell on them in power.

How we need to follow their example in our day. Is it possible that the presence of the Holy Spirit is not evident in our midst because we do not follow the example of the early church? Are we willing to commit ourselves to seeking the Lord in prayer and obedience to his Word? Are we willing to cast aside our own ideas and wait expectantly for God to reveal his will? May the Lord cause us to follow the example of this early church.

For Consideration:

- Consider the characteristics of the early church as described here in this passage. How does your church measure up? How do you measure up personally?

- Are there areas in your life where you need to be obedient? What are they? What hinders you from being obedient right now?

- Have you ever found yourself doubting the Lord? What is the challenge of this passage to you today?

- Do you need to see a fresh move of God's Spirit in your life or in your church? What do you need to do as you wait?

For Prayer:

- As you consider the characteristics of the early disciples in this passage, ask the Lord to show you if you have failed in any way to follow their example.

- Ask the Lord to forgive you for the times when you have not been obedient. Ask him to give you courage and strength to be obedient.

- Ask the Lord to give you patience as you wait on him.

- Commit your local church to the Lord in prayer. Pray that each of the characteristics we examined in this passage will be demonstrated in your church as well.

- Ask the Lord to fill you more and more with his Spirit, enabling you to be an even greater witness.

3

The Coming of the Holy Spirit

Read Acts 2:1–13

I t was the day of the Jewish festival of Pentecost. Jews from everywhere came to Jerusalem to celebrate this special day. The followers of Jesus had gathered separately. While they were together, the Holy Spirit came to them. Notice here that they heard his coming. The Bible tells us that they heard a sound like a violent wind. There was something strange about this wind. Luke tells us that it came from heaven and filled the house where the disciples had gathered. Though this wind was violent, these disciples knew that it was heaven-sent. They were aware that God was doing something in their midst.

These believers also saw tongues of fire (verse 3). As they watched, these tongues of fire began to separate and "rest" individually on each person present in the room. While their experience was corporate, it was also very personal. Each believer was individually filled with the presence of the Holy Spirit. This should not go unnoticed. You may be part of a church where the Spirit of God is moving, but this is not enough. You must know a personal filling yourself.

Notice the result of the filling of the Holy Spirit. Verse 4 tells us that they spoke in other tongues as the Spirit enabled them. The phrase "as the Spirit enabled them" is significant. This phrase teaches us that this speaking in tongues was only possible because of the Spirit's work in their lives. What took place that day was of a spiritual nature. It was a direct result of the ministry of the Holy Spirit in the lives of these believers.

While it is often assumed that everyone present that day spoke in tongues, this is not clear from the passage. While they were all filled with the Holy Spirit, they only spoke in tongues as the Spirit enabled them.

It appears from verse 6 that when the Spirit came to them that day things got rather noisy. People from all around came to see what was going on. Before this, they appear to be unnoticed. When their neighbors arrived, they heard "the wonders of God" in their own language (verse 11). Verses 9–10 give us a list of the various languages that were spoken that day. It appears that the Holy Spirit gave to these believers the ability to proclaim the wonders of God in the languages of the people who had come to Jerusalem for Pentecost. This gift had an evangelistic thrust. It was given so that unbelievers could hear the message of salvation in their own languages.

Some Christians today understand this passage to be saying that God gave a gift of interpretation to the unsaved who were listening. There are several problems with this interpretation. The passage does not say that the unbelievers were given a gift to interpret the languages that were spoken. If anything, it tells us that they heard these words in their own languages. The gift was given to believers, not to unbelievers. The passage is quite clear that believers did actually speak in other languages and that they did so enabled by the Holy Spirit.

The gift of tongues in Acts 2 seems to be different from the gift mentioned by Paul in 1 Corinthians 14. The gift of Acts 2 appears to be the ability to communicate the Word of God in a known language. No interpretation of these tongues was required for the unsaved to understand. The gift of 1 Corinthians 14 was different. Paul said that those who use this gift do not speak to people but to God. Paul also said that no one can understand this kind of tongues without an interpreter: "For anyone who speaks in a tongue does not speak to men but to God. Indeed, no one understands him; he utters mysteries with his spirit" (1 Corinthians 14:2).

The gift of tongues in 1 Corinthians 14 was for the edification of the individual using the gift and, under special circumstances, for the church as well. In Acts 2 the gift had an evangelistic thrust and was intended to clearly present the gospel to those who came to Jerusalem for Pentecost.

In Acts 1:8 Jesus had promised his disciples that the Holy Spirit would come on them to enable them to be his witnesses. This is exactly what was happening in Acts 2. The Holy Spirit came to the followers of Christ and immediately they boldly spoke out the message of the gospel.

Notice the response of the people. Some were amazed at what they heard. This amazement may have been in part because they heard the message of the gospel in their own language. They were also astonished, however, to hear these believers so boldly proclaim the wonders of God. They recognized a supernatural power at work and cried out, "What does this mean"? (verse 12). This first group did not understand. They needed to understand before they could truly believe.

The second group made fun of the believers. They did not see the hand of God at work in what took place that day. They attributed these manifestations to drunkenness. These individuals turned their backs on the work of the Holy Spirit in their midst.

Those on whom the Spirit fell, however, knew the significance of what was taking place. They knew his empowering. I wonder what my response would have been if I had been among the crowd that day? There are really three groups of people represented in this passage of Scripture. First, there are those who stand at a distance and wonder. Second, there are those who want nothing to do with what they see and mock the work of the Spirit of God. Third, there are those who experience first-hand the Spirit's filling and empowering.

The experience of this filling and empowering of the Holy Spirit can and must be ours as well. Paul tells us in Romans: "You, however, are controlled not by the sinful nature but by the Spirit, if the Spirit of God lives in you. And if anyone does not have the Spirit of Christ, he does not belong to Christ" (Romans 8:9). Paul tells us here that the filling of the Spirit is the normal experience of Christians. Is there evidence that God is at work in our lives? The same Spirit who came to the early church desires to empower us today. Without him, we can do nothing of lasting spiritual value.

We have all too often cast the Holy Spirit aside. We are afraid of what he will do in our lives. Isn't it time we stopped running from God's Spirit? Isn't it time we surrendered to what he wants to do in us? Without the ministry of the Holy Spirit, we are destined to a powerless and lifeless faith. In his Spirit alone there is power.

For Consideration:

• What evidence is there in your life that you are filled with the Holy Spirit?

- What happens to the believers at Pentecost when the Holy Spirit comes to them? Is there evidence of this in your life?

- What fears do you have of total surrender to the work and ministry of the Holy Spirit?

For Prayer:

- Ask the Lord to fill you with his Spirit so that his boldness and power might be clearly seen in your life.

- Ask God to reveal anything that might stand in the way of his Spirit working in your life.

- Thank the Lord that he has promised his Holy Spirit to all who belong to him.

4

The Fulfillment of Prophecy

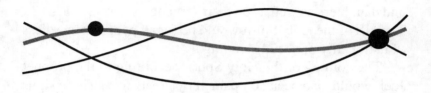

Read Acts 2:14–21

The apostle Peter appears to have been the leader among the apostles. When he saw the confusion of the Jews in regard to what was taking place that day, he stood up and addressed the crowd. He explained to them that these occurrences were not of human origin. The apostles were not drunk, as some had insinuated, because it was still very early in the morning. What they were seeing before them was a fulfillment of the prophecy of Joel.

Let's look at Joel's prophecy in light of what was taking place in Acts 2. Joel tells us that in the last days, God would pour out his Spirit on all flesh. In Scripture the term "last days" refers to the time after the coming of the Messiah. We are living in the last days now. What Joel is telling us is that in the days after the appearance of the Messiah, God's Spirit would be poured out on people.

Notice that the outpouring of the Spirit of God would be on all people (verse 17). In other words, the outpouring of the Spirit of God would not be only on those of Jewish nationality but on all nations. This is what the disciples were experiencing in Acts 2. They were proclaiming the "wonders of God" in the languages of many nations. People from many nationalities were hearing in their own languages the message of salvation for the first time. With the coming of the Messiah, the message of the gospel would be presented to the entire world in the power of the Holy Spirit.

Joel also prophesied that the Holy Spirit would be no respecter of persons. He would be poured out on their sons and daughters as well as on their servants (see verses 17–18). The gift of the Holy Spirit would be for all people, regardless of nationality or social standing.

The coming of the Holy Spirit, according to the prophet Joel, would also be accompanied by great signs. These signs can be divided into two types. First, there would be the signs of prophecy, visions, and dreams. This was nothing new for the Jews. The Jews understood that there were those who had been gifted of God in prophecy. They held the writings of the Old Testament prophets in high regard. Dreams and visions were very much a part of the Old Testament culture. Joseph and Jacob had dreams from God, and Isaiah, Jeremiah, and Daniel had visions from God.

In Joel's prophecy, however, the average person would be experiencing these dreams, visions, and prophecies. It was not only the religious leadership who would experience these dreams and visions but also the common man or woman. Jewish sons and daughters would prophesy. Old men would experience dreams from the Lord. Young men would see visions. Even the servants in their households would prophesy like the prophets of the Old Testament. The Spirit of God would come to the common person as he had come to the religious leadership of the Old Testament. The lowest servant in their households would stand up and speak a word from the Lord under the inspiration of the Spirit of God. This was something new.

Joel also foretold wonders in the heavens and signs on the earth (verse 19). Joel prophesied that in the days after the coming of Messiah, the earth would see blood, fire, and billows of smoke. The sun would be turned to darkness and the moon to blood before the coming of the final day of the Lord. One only has to read the book of Revelation to see that this is exactly what the apostle John predicted would happen before the return of the Lord Jesus. The days of the end will not be easy days. The earth will indeed see much bloodshed and violence. Fire will destroy the earth. The sun itself will be destroyed. These signs are yet to appear.

In the meantime, the Spirit of God has been poured out on the common person. Through ordinary men and women like you and me, the message of salvation is going to the ends of the earth. Joel reminds us here that anyone who calls on the name of the Lord will be saved. We do not have to perish. The first signs would be warning signs. The second signs would be judgment signs. Today God speaks to us as he spoke to the people gathered in Jerusalem for the Pentecost. Tomorrow the blood, fire, and smoke may be on us. Will we be ready? The prophecy of Joel has already begun to see its fulfillment. It will not be long before it sees its complete fulfillment in the judgment of this earth.

On the day of Pentecost, Peter reminded the people gathered before him that the coming of the Holy Spirit was the beginning of the fulfillment of the great prophecy of Joel. He challenged them to make themselves ready for the final day of the Lord. Their only hope lay in the Lord himself. Only by calling out to him could they be saved from the wrath to come. The people gathered that day in Jerusalem were very religious people. After all, they had come to Jerusalem to worship God. It was, however, to these people that the apostle Peter brought his message of renewal and hope. Maybe you too are a very religious person like these Jews. You need to hear this message. Your religion will not save you in the day of the Lord's appearance. Only those who call on the Lord will be saved.

For Consideration:

- What evidence is there of the work of the Spirit of God in our midst?

- Are we living in the last days? What evidence is there of this?

- What does it mean to call on the name of the Lord?

For Prayer:

- Thank the Lord for his Spirit.

- Ask forgiveness for the times that you have not been responsive to the work of the Spirit of God in your life.

- Pray that God may have full control of your life through the ministry of his Spirit in your heart.

5

This Man Jesus

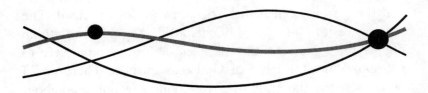

Read Acts 2:22–41

We have seen that the ministry of the Holy Spirit is to point men and women to Christ (1:8). This is exactly what was happening in this passage. Having been filled with the Holy Spirit, the apostle Peter stood up to speak to the crowd. The central focus of his message was the person of Jesus Christ. Let us examine in detail what Peter had to say about Jesus in his sermon.

Jesus was a man accredited by God (verse 22)

Peter told his listeners that Jesus was a man "accredited by God" to them by means of the miracles, wonders, and signs. Peter appears to be telling his listeners that the miracles of Jesus had a very particular purpose. These miracles proved beyond a shadow of a doubt that the Lord Jesus was indeed sent by the Father. Listen to what Jesus himself said: "I have testimony weightier than that of John. For the very work that the Father has given me to finish, and which I am doing, testifies that the Father has sent me" (John 5:36). Again Jesus said to the people who refused to believe in him: "Do not believe me unless I do what my Father does. But if I do it, even though you do not believe me, believe the miracles, that you may know and understand that the Father is in me, and I in the Father" (John 10:37–38).

Our Lord performed miracles to prove that he ministered in the power of God himself. There is no other explanation for the great miracles of Jesus. Here was a man who had the power to command nature itself. Here was a man who had the power to heal the sick and to raise the dead. The very power of God was at his disposal. Any person with an open mind looking at the miracles of Jesus would have to recognize that the hand of God was on him. There could be no doubt in the mind of anyone who saw and read about the ministry of Jesus that he was approved by God and ministered in his power.

He was handed over by God's purpose (verse 23)

It would have been easy for Peter's listeners to say that if Jesus was really approved by God, why did he die such a cruel death? Peter went on to say that even the death of Jesus was in God's overall purpose. While wicked men nailed our Lord Jesus to the cross, God, in his great sovereign plan, chose to use this human evil to bring about the salvation of his people. Have you ever had something tragic happen to you? Be encouraged by this verse. God can take what appears to be a great tragedy and use it to accomplish much good in your life.

God raised him from the dead (verse 24)

While it appeared that the cross was a great victory for the enemies of the Lord Jesus, in reality the opposite was true. After the cross came the resurrection. Peter reminded his listeners that the grave could not hold the Lord Jesus.

The Lord Jesus broke the chains of death. Peter pointed his audience to the book of Psalms to prove that what he was saying concerning the Lord Jesus was prophesied long before it happened. He reminded them of Psalm 16:8–11 where David said that the "Holy One" would not see decay. Jesus' body did not decay (Psalm 16:10). After three days Jesus had risen from the dead. Everyone listening to Peter had heard about this. The fact that death could not hold the Lord Jesus was proof that he was God. Will you notice the encouragement that the Psalmist took from the fact that death could not hold the Holy One. David was quoted as saying that because the Lord was always before him, he could not be shaken (verse 25). He stated that because God could not see corruption, he had great assurance.

Our friends and loved ones will one day pass on. They will not always be here with us. This is not so with God. The eternal God will always remain. He will always be here with us and for us. Nothing can shake us as long as God exists. He is always before us as a God who has overcome death and evil.

Furthermore, the Psalmist was referenced as saying that because the Holy One could not see corruption, his body could "live in hope" (verse 26). Because God lives, he could live as well. The fact that God had overcome death means that in him we too can overcome it. Our hope is in him. God would not let his Holy One see decay. While this ultimately was a prophecy about the Lord Jesus, the Psalmist took personal encouragement in the hope that he too would eventually be raised from death.

For the believer there is great hope. If death could not keep our Savior neither will it keep those who are in him. This thought caused the Psalmist to break forth into rejoicing. He had every reason to rejoice. His heart rejoiced in the knowledge that he would one day be filled with joy in the very presence of his Lord. Death was not the end for him. He would see God and rejoice in his presence.

Peter reminded his audience that the fulfillment of this prophecy of David was found in the Lord Jesus alone (verses 29–31). David himself had died. His body was in the tomb. His body had decayed in the grave. He could not possibly be the one whose body would not see corruption. This could only be said of the Lord Jesus. His body was no longer in the tomb. Peter's listeners were well aware of this fact. Peter and all the disciples present that day were witnesses to the fact that Jesus was alive. They had seen him with their own eyes.

He was exalted to the right hand of God (verse 33)

Not only had Jesus risen from the dead, he was also, according to Peter, exalted by God (verse 33). This Jesus who was crucified is Lord and Christ. While he was Lord before he came to this earth, his death on the cross officially established this lordship. His death and resurrection were the official seals of his lordship over sin, death, and Satan. As Lord, he is now exalted at the right hand of the Father. The right hand symbolizes fellowship and favor. Jesus sits at the right hand of the Father because it is the will of the Father to exalt him.

Peter mentioned yet another prophecy of David in this context: "The LORD says to my Lord: 'Sit at my right hand until I make your enemies a footstool for your feet'" (Psalm 110:1). Peter saw in this prophecy of David a clear reference to the exaltation of Christ. God the Father spoke here to God the Son. The Father called the Son to sit at his right hand. He promised the Son that all his enemies would be his footstool. God the Father was saying that he would place all the enemies of Christ under his feet. They would become his subjects. Christ would be Lord over his greatest enemies. He would be Lord of all.

Peter's message was very simple. Jesus was approved by God. He died according to God's particular purpose. He rose from the dead and was glorified at the side of the Father. When the crowd heard the message, they were so moved that they cried out: "Brothers, what shall we do?" (verse 37). What were they saying? They had heard a clear presentation of the gospel. The Holy Spirit of God was moving among them. They knew that they needed to respond to Peter's message. The Holy Spirit was calling them to respond. They realized their guilt in rejecting and crucifying the Lord Jesus. They knew they were sinners. It was for this reason that they cried out: "What shall we do?"

Peter did not hesitate to tell them what they were to do. First, they were to repent (verse 38). Repentance requires two steps. The first step is to recognize sin and confess it to God. The second step is to turn from sin and practice it no more. What Peter was telling the Jews was that they were to recognize their guilt, confess it, and turn away from their evil ways.

The second thing they were to do was to be baptized in the name of the Lord Jesus. What is the significance of baptism? Baptism is a symbol of our identification with Christ. Not only were these Jews to repent but they were also to commit themselves to living and serving the Lord Jesus. Their baptism publicly identified them with Jesus Christ. They were not to be ashamed to be called by his name. They were to publicly profess him as Lord.

Peter went on to explain the result of repentance and identification with Christ. First, if his listeners repented of their sins and turned their lives over to the Lord Jesus, they would be forgiven. It does not matter how big our sins are. If we confess them, we can be forgiven. Perhaps among these individuals that day were men and women who had shouted, "Crucify him! Crucify him!" when Pilate had asked them what they wanted him to do with Jesus (John 19:6, 19). They knew that they had crucified the Lord. Peter was giving them hope. They could be forgiven despite the horrible nature of their sin.

The second promise was that if they confessed their sins and turned their lives over to Christ, they would receive the Holy Spirit. That Holy Spirit would lead them to truth and empower them in service for Christ. He would convict them of their sins and make them everything that God wanted them to be. Jesus would not leave them to fend for themselves.

Peter reminded them that the promises of forgiveness and the gift of the Holy Spirit were not only for them but for all whom the Lord would call. If their children or "all who are far off" heard the call of the Lord, repented of their sins, and turned their lives over to him, they too could know his forgiveness and the power of the promised Holy Spirit in their lives (verse 39). This good news was for all people.

When the people heard these words, they were convicted in their hearts. Three thousand individuals were baptized that day. God was beginning a great work in their midst. What is particularly striking in this passage is the simplicity of the message and the power in which it went forth. While the words were simple, they were empowered by the Holy Spirit. I am sure that Peter and the believers present that day were astonished at what they saw before them. They were seeing the fulfillment of the wonderful promise of the coming of the Holy Spirit to empower the church. This was a new experience for them. They were only beginning to understand the incredible power they had at their disposal to do battle with the enemy.

For Consideration:

• What do we learn here about the person of Christ?

• What was it about the message of Peter that so powerfully touched the lives of those present that day?

- Do we see this type of preaching in our day?

- Do you know something of this empowering in your ministry and life? What is the difference between ministering in the flesh and ministering in the Spirit?

For Prayer:

- Review what Peter tells us about the person of Christ. Take a moment to thank Christ for who he is.

- Ask the Lord to raise up in our day preachers like Peter, who are empowered not by human wisdom but by the Spirit of God.

- Pray for this empowering in the life of your own pastor and church leaders.

6

The Early Church

Read Acts 2:42–47

P eter's sermon on the day of Pentecost touched many lives. Three thousand individuals were added to the church as a result of the Spirit-filled preaching of the apostle. There was nothing counterfeit about these early believers. They were not caught up in the emotion of a moment. Their conversion was genuine. Their lives were dramatically changed. A quick look at this passage shows us the nature of the change that took place in the church because of what the Spirit of God did on the day of Pentecost.

They devoted themselves to the apostles' teaching

For these three thousand believers, everything was new. As babes in Christ, they needed instruction in the ways of the Lord. This passage tells us that the followers of Christ devoted themselves to the teaching of the apostles. Let us consider this in detail.

First, this devotion implied that they took the time to

listen to what the apostles had to say. You cannot devote yourselves to a particular teaching if you have never taken the time to examine that teaching. These people spent many hours under the instruction of the apostles. We will discover that many of these believers were instructed daily in the Word of God.

Devotion to the teaching of the apostles implied much more than simple instruction. These believers also committed themselves to living that teaching in their daily lives. The word devotion implies perseverance and diligent application. What they learned from the apostles was put into practice in their lives. Here was a church that committed itself not only to the study of the Word of God but also its daily application.

They devoted themselves to fellowship

Disciples in the early church were also devoted to fellowship. Their commitment was not only upward to God but also outward to their brothers and sisters in Christ. The word "fellowship" in the Greek language refers to a partnership. We see in these verses how this partnership with their brothers and sisters worked itself out: "All the believers were together and had everything in common. Selling their possessions and goods, they gave to anyone as he had need" (verses 44–45).

There is some confusion as to the meaning of the phrase "all believers were together." We might take from this that these people lived together in some form of community. We might also see this in the sense of the believers being of one heart toward each other. What is clear is that when these disciples spoke of "sharing," they did not mean telling their brother or sister in Christ their most recent news. To these believers, fellowship implied a willingness to sell what they had to provide for a brother or sister who had a greater need. They did not consider what they had to be theirs alone.

Everything they had was devoted to the Lord and to their fellow believers. There is no indication that this practice was forced on the community. The context implies that they willingly gave up their possessions for each other. Because of what happened at Pentecost, there was a radical change in the priorities of these new disciples.

What a challenge this is to us today. We do not need to sell everything we own and give it to the church, but we do need to examine ourselves in light of what we see in the early church. These individuals did not feel it a burden to give everything they had to the Lord. What should our response be when we see a brother in need? We must admire the commitment of these people to each other. This is clearly an evidence of the working of the Spirit of God in their midst.

Paul told the Philippians: "Do nothing out of selfish ambition or vain conceit, but in humility consider others better than yourselves. Each of you should look not only to your own interests, but also to the interests of others. Your attitude should be the same as that of Christ Jesus" (Philippians 2:3–5). Does this describe your relationship with the body of Christ? Are you, like this early church, willing to put someone else's interests above your own?

They devoted themselves to the breaking of bread

The "breaking of bread" here very likely refers to the Lord's Supper. Verse 46 seems to join the breaking of bread with the practice of eating together in homes. There is evidence in Scripture that would lead us to understand that the Lord's Supper was part of a much larger meal. Paul rebuked the believers in Corinth because they were abusing this meal: "When you come together, it is not the Lord's Supper you eat, for as you eat, each of you goes ahead without waiting for anybody else. One remains hungry, another gets drunk" (1 Corinthians 11:20–21). It is evident from this that the "breaking of bread" was in the context of a community meal in Corinth.

It was in the context of a common meal together with his disciples that Jesus instituted the Lord's Supper. It is quite likely that the early church continued this practice of having the Lord's Supper during their regular community meals. What is important for us to see is not how the early church practiced the Lord's Supper but that the church had devoted itself to remembering the death and resurrection of their Lord in this way.

The Lord's Supper gives us an opportunity to reflect on what our Savior has done for us. We need to be a people who always have his death and resurrection before our eyes. The Lord's Supper is a time for personal reflection (1 Corinthians 11:27–28). These disciples in the early church regularly took a spiritual inventory of their lives by means of the Lord's Supper. Were they living in a manner worthy of the Lord Jesus? Were they in a right relationship with him as their Savior? Were they in a right relationship with their brothers and sisters in Christ? Was there anything that had crept into their lives to hinder their relationship with their God? These were questions that they would have to ask themselves every time they came together for the breaking of bread.

We all need these times of reflection. The Lord has given us the Lord's Supper as a means of reflection on these vital issues. In our age of rushing from one thing to another, we usually do not take the time to do a spiritual inventory of our lives. The Lord's Supper provides us with this time. This is not something we should rush through. It can become for us a very meaningful time. The early church was devoted to this practice of the Lord's Supper and the personal examination it required in light of the death and resurrection of the Lord Jesus.

They devoted themselves to prayer

We see also that this early church was devoted to prayer. What is prayer? Prayer is communion with God (Psalm 62:8). It includes many dimensions. Prayer provides us first with the means of expressing our gratitude and worship to God (Matthew 11:25). This is what we see happening in verse 47. Furthermore, by prayer we recognize our need of God and his enabling (Psalm 34:6). We bring our burdens and requests to him, understanding that he alone can answer our needs. By prayer, the early church confessed shortcomings and acknowledged a need of God in these shortcomings. Moreover, prayer provides a means by which we can hear God speak to us. As we sit before him in quietness, his Spirit speaks to our spirit (Acts 13:2–3). We are comforted and encouraged through prayer. Here was a group of disciples devoted to prayer in its many dimensions. By prayer, they were committed to expressing thanksgiving and worship to God. By prayer, they recognized their need of his intervention in their lives. By prayer, they quieted their hearts to listen to what God might say to them.

We see in this section the fourfold devotion of the early church: the teaching of the apostles, fellowship, the breaking of bread, and prayer. What was the result of this devotion in the life of the early church? It is clear that this devotion bore wonderful fruit.

Powerful evidence of the presence of the Holy Spirit

There was in the life of this church a very powerful evidence of the working of the Holy Spirit. Verse 43 tells us that everyone was filled with awe. There was a sense of the presence of the Lord in their midst. People were amazed at what the Lord was doing. The followers of Christ were aware that what was taking place that day was supernatural. God was moving among them. Even the unsaved people around them would have seen these powerful demonstrations of the Holy Spirit. The result was that the church enjoyed "the favor of all the people" (verse 47).

Furthermore, many wonders and miraculous signs were being done by the apostles as a sign of the powerful work of the Holy Spirit in their midst. We have already seen in verse 22 of this chapter that the Lord Jesus was accredited to the world by means of miraculous signs. The apostles were also given this power. The purpose of these miracles and signs was to prove to the world that these men were truly from God. There was no other explanation for what was taking place that day.

Yet a further evidence of the moving of the Spirit of God in their midst was the fact that these disciples were found every day in the temple court (verse 46). They were not content with "Sunday Christianity." So great was their hunger for the Word of God that every day they were found in the presence of God's people listening to his Word and worshiping their Lord. Other things were pushed aside. There was nothing they wanted more than to be with God's people. The only explanation for this was that the Holy Spirit of God was moving in revival power among them.

Notice finally that these believers ate together with glad and sincere hearts. The Greek word used here is interesting. The word used here for sincere means "smooth" or "single." In this context it means that there were no rough edges in their relationships with each other. They had a single mind. They were not double-faced in their relationships with each other. How often have we longed to find such a church? Problems among Christians abound. One of the greatest evidences of the moving of the Spirit in the early church was the healing of relationships. Where there is healing of personal relationships, there is gladness of heart. This was the experience of these early disciples.

The Lord added to their number daily

As many unsaved individuals looked at what the Lord was doing in the lives of his people, they were struck by the evidence of the power of God (verse 47). These followers of Christ enjoyed the favor of all people. There was nothing evil that could be said of them. The unbeliever was powerless before this practical demonstration of God's power. One by one the unbelievers were being broken by the testimony of the church and the working of the Holy Spirit. Every day people were added to the church.

God's Spirit was moving in power in the midst of his people. How we long to see him move in this way in our own lives. May God grant to us the privilege of seeing this in our day.

For Consideration:

- How does our modern church compare to the church of Pentecost? Give examples.

- Review the characteristics of this early church. How do you personally compare to these early Christians?

- How do you explain what happened in the early church? What would have to change for us to see this in our day?

For Prayer

- Ask the Lord to change us today so that we might experience something of what God was doing in the early church.

- Do you have relationships that are broken in your life? Ask the Lord to bring healing to those relationships.

- Ask God to increase your devotion to his Word, to prayer, to fellow Christians, and to remembering what Christ has done for you.

7

An Extended Hand

Read Acts 3:1–10

We have already seen that it was the custom of the early church to meet on a daily basis in the temple. On one of those occasions when Peter and John were going to the temple, they met a lame man at the gate. It appears that this man had been placed there every day so that he could beg for money. Could it be that the believers passed him every day as they went to the temple? On this occasion, as Peter and John passed by, the beggar asked them for money. Both disciples looked directly at the man. Peter told him that while he did not have any silver or gold, he did have something of even greater value. With that, he told the lame man to walk in the name of the Lord Jesus (verse 6).

Notice that Peter then extended his hand to the man (verse 7). This should not go unnoticed. There is a very valuable lesson for us. Peter had just commanded the man to rise up and walk in the name of the Lord Jesus. Nothing else should have been required. The Lord Jesus could have healed the man without any further action on the part of Peter. What is interesting to note, however, is that the man was not healed until Peter took him by the hand and helped him to his feet.

What would have happened if Peter had not extended his hand to this man? We can only guess. Would this man have simply laughed at Peter? Would he have let his logic tell him that Peter was talking nonsense? The experience of this lame beggar told him that he could not possibly have stood on his feet. What was the use of trying? He knew what the result would be. If it were possible for him to get up and walk, he surely would not have been begging for money at the temple gate. Maybe realizing what was going through this man's mind, Peter extended his hand to him and began to pull him to his feet.

With Peter's help, the man began to use his muscles. Maybe the faith inside him was being stirred. Could this be real? Would God actually heal him? To the beggar's utter surprise, he felt strength coming to his legs and ankles. He stood up. He was healed. This was nothing short of a miracle. Had Peter not taken him by the hand and started to pull him to his feet, how long would he have sat on his mat?

There are many people like this beggar. Maybe they are in need of salvation. For years they have heard the truth but have never responded. Like this disabled man, they need someone to extend a hand to them. Your hand may be all it would take to break the chains and set them free.

There is no doubt that the power of Christ is sufficient to heal and release, but there are times when that healing will not take place until we extend our hand to the person in need. Maybe all it would take is for you to invite someone to a Bible study or prayer meeting. Maybe someone needs to see a believer extend a hand in a very practical way to minister to a particular need. Maybe it means simply going to a person and speaking about your faith. One thing is certain, many people will not respond until they see your extended hand. This by no means diminishes the power of God to heal. It simply means that God has chosen to work in partnership with us in the task of reaching this world with the message of the gospel.

Let me say one thing more about this extending of the hand. By extending his hand, Peter had to sincerely believe what he claimed. Many times we do not extend a hand because we are afraid that it will do no good. What use would there be for Peter to extend his hand if he did not believe that in so doing the Lord would bring healing to this man? Like Peter, we must also believe that God can indeed do a work in the lives of the people to whom we extend our hands.

Notice the result of Peter extending his hand. Even as he was being helped to his feet, the man who had been lame from birth experienced the power of God at work in his life. He jumped to his feet. He walked on his own. He knew that God had touched his life. He went with the disciples into the temple to worship God. He was so full of praise that he could not contain himself. Right there in the temple court he jumped for joy and shouted praise to God (verse 8). He was not concerned about what others would think. His eyes were on the God who had healed him.

The people in the temple that day recognized him as the one who had been at the temple gate. They were amazed at the power of God. What a day it must have been! The believers who had gathered for worship had much for which to praise God. God himself had met with them that day in the person of the crippled beggar. It all happened because Peter had reached out his hand in faith. What would happen if you reached out your hand to someone today?

For Consideration:

- What is your church presently doing to "extend a hand" to those in need in your community? What are you doing personally?

- What kind of things can you do in your community to extend a hand to someone in need?

For Prayer:

- Ask the Lord to give you someone to whom you can personally extend a hand. Ask him what it is you can do for that person to lead them closer to the Savior.

- Thank the Lord that he has chosen to work through weak individuals like you and me.

8

Introducing the Healer

Read Acts 3:11–26

The lame man who had sat at the temple gate had just been healed. This had caused quite a stir among the people who had gathered for worship that day. They had seen the man begging for money outside the temple gate. Maybe some had tossed a few coins into his hands as they had entered the temple. People came running from all directions to see for themselves what had happened.

When they arrived, they saw the beggar holding on to Peter and John. Why was he holding on to the apostles? It was certainly not because his healing was incomplete. We see in verse 8 that he was fully able to walk and jump. In verse 16 Peter tells us that this man's healing was complete. It is also evident from the astonishment of the people present that this man was completely healed. It seems, therefore, more likely that the reason this man was holding on to Peter and John was because of his deep appreciation for what they had done for him.

Peter could not let this opportunity pass. He clearly had the attention of the crowd. Verse 12 tells us that the people stared at Peter and John as though they were superhuman in nature. It was as though the crowd expected them to speak.

Peter began his speech by saying that they should not really be surprised at what had taken place. He reminded them that the power for this miracle was not to be found in them, as mere men, but in Jesus Christ. They were simply channels through which that power could flow. Two things merit mentioning here.

First, notice the expectation on the part of the apostles. They truly expected that the power of the Lord Jesus would flow through them. Was this not what the Lord had promised before he returned to heaven? The apostles were not surprised that the Lord was true to his promise.

Second, notice the humility and integrity of the apostles. Peter was very quick to tell those who had gathered the truth about this miracle. The power to heal this lame beggar was from God and God alone. Peter realized that he could never have healed the man on his own. All the glory for this miracle belonged to the Lord.

Before going any further with this passage, let's consider what we have been speaking about in more detail. Do you expect the Lord's power to flow through you? Do you expect that the Lord will do something great through your life? Are you surprised to see that the Holy Spirit works through you to touch someone else? If we are honest with ourselves, many of us have to admit that we do not have great expectations for our lives and our spiritual impact on those around us. When we understand, however, that the power within us is the very power of God, we will live our lives expecting great things from him.

When we see the Lord working in our lives, what is our reaction? Is it not human to try to keep some of that glory for ourselves? We like to think that somehow we have had a part to play also. This was not the attitude of Peter. We must admire the humility of this man who turned the attention of the onlookers away from himself to the Lord.

Finding the balance between expectation and humility is not always easy, but it is here that we must live. We should not be surprised that God would do something great in our lives, but we must always be honest in recognizing the source of that power. Peter drew the attention of the people away from himself and placed it where it rightly belonged. Let's look at what Peter told the onlookers about the Lord Jesus in verses 13–15.

He was glorified by God (verse 13)

Some of these onlookers may have been responsible for handing Jesus over to be crucified. Pilate had wanted to set him free, but the crowd had persisted in seeking his crucifixion. The Jews had disowned Jesus before the world. After his horrible death on the cross, the Lord Jesus was raised from the dead and given a place of honor at the right hand of God. His power had just been demonstrated in the life of the beggar who stood before them. No one could deny that a miracle had taken place.

He is the Holy and Righteous One (verse 14)

Peter told his listeners that Jesus was the Holy and Righteous One. This reference to the Holy and Righteous One is a clear reference to the Messiah. Romans 3:10 tells us that there is no one who is righteous. All of us have fallen short of God's standard of righteousness. There is only one person who rightly deserves this title. The Lord Jesus Christ alone met God's standard of righteousness. He alone is the Holy and Righteous One. The Jews present that day would have seen in this title a reference to the Messiah. Peter was telling them that they had crucified the Messiah. There was real boldness on the part of Peter. He had no way of knowing what the reaction of the people would be to this statement.

He is the author of life (verse 15)

Peter stated that the Lord Jesus is the author of life. He is the author of spiritual life and he is also the author of physical life. The apostle John tells us that all things were made through the Lord Jesus (John 1:3). This very clearly reminds us that Jesus is God. The author of life was willing to lay down his life so that we might have life for all eternity. It was not at all surprising for Peter that the author of life could bring healing to the legs of a lame man.

Peter then applied his message to the needs of his audience. While he stated that these people had acted in ignorance in killing the Lord Jesus (verse 16), he told them to repent of the sin of rebellion and turn to God. He reminded them that their rebellion against the Holy One was prophesied long ago. He pointed them to the prophecies of the suffering Messiah. In so doing, he reminded them that they were the ones who had caused his suffering. If they repented and turned to God, a time of healing and refreshing could still be theirs (verse 19). What a wonderful example of the grace of our Lord Jesus. Those who had been responsible for his suffering and death were now being offered forgiveness and full pardon.

Peter next reminded his listeners that the Lord Jesus would return again. At that time he would restore everything to his Father (verse 21). Satan has done much damage in this world. He has turned many away from God. The time is coming, however, when the Lord Jesus will destroy all his works (Hebrews 2:14–15; 1 John 3:8). The healing of the lame man was but a small foretaste of the power of the Lord Jesus to break the chains of darkness.

Peter warned the people of the dangers of refusing this wonderful offer of forgiveness. Moses had prophesied the coming of the Lord Jesus and had given this warning: "Anyone who does not listen to him will be completely cut off from among his people" (verse 23). Eternal separation from God was the destiny of those who refused this offer.

Peter told those present that day that they were without excuse before God (verses 24–26). God had spared no effort to tell his people of his great plan of salvation. Repeatedly he had spoken to his people through the prophets and now he had spoken through his Son. Peter pleaded with his listeners to turn to the Lord Jesus.

Now is the time for us to make things right. When Jesus returns again it will be too late. The miracle of this chapter serves to draw attention to the Lord Jesus. It proves to us that he is alive and that his promises are true.

For Consideration:

• Consider how Peter took advantage of this opportunity to share Christ. How can we prepare ourselves to take advantage of opportunities to share Christ?

• Why do you think we are content with mediocrity in our Christian lives?

• Why is it so hard to believe that God can and will do great things through us?

• What does this chapter teach us about humility?

For Prayer:

• Ask the Lord to reveal his power more abundantly in your life.

• Ask him to help you to always give him the glory for what he is doing through your ministry for him.

- Ask him for victory over pride and false humility, which take glory away from the Lord Jesus and keep us from stepping out boldly to do great things for him.

9

Before the Sanhedrin

Read Acts 4:1–23

We have been examining the healing of the lame beggar. This miracle had given Peter the opportunity to preach the gospel to those assembled in the temple that afternoon. We have not yet seen the impact that this miracle had on the city of Jerusalem.

The religious leaders were among those listening to Peter that day. The Sadducees, in particular, were not pleased to hear Peter speak about the resurrection of the Lord Jesus. Matthew 22:23 tells us that the Sadducees did not believe in the resurrection of the dead. They decided to seize both Peter and John and put them in jail.

What is important for us to notice is the impact of Peter's message. Verse 4 tells us that many people believed. That day the number of believers increased to five thousand. We understand from Acts 2:41 that the number of disciples before this was about three thousand. We should not assume, however, that two thousand people came to the Lord because of the healing of the lame man. From Acts 2:47 we understand that since Pentecost, souls were being added to the church on a daily basis. While we do not know how many people came to know the Lord that day, we can be sure that the number was significant. Who would have thought that the beggar sitting at the entrance of the temple would be the instrument God would use to bring so many people into his kingdom? This miracle had a profound impact on the city of Jerusalem.

The religious leaders were very much aware of the impact the apostles were having on the people. In just a short time, their followers had grown from just over one hundred to over five thousand. This posed a serious threat to the Jewish leaders. Something had to be done to stop the spread of Christianity. The next day, all the important religious officials gathered to discuss the problem. Peter and John were brought before them and asked to give an account of their actions.

Peter and John were aware of the seriousness of the situation. Not long before this, they had stood before a fire warming their hands while this same council was questioning their Lord. This very group had condemned Jesus to death and would certainly not hesitate to pass the same sentence on his apostles.

Was it not ironic that Peter then stood in the same place as his master? The last time he had seen this council was when the Lord Jesus was standing before them. At that time, he had denied the Lord three times. Was this going through his mind as he stood there that day? How would he respond this time? Would he break under the pressure, as he had the last time?

Peter, filled with the Spirit, stood boldly before the council and unashamedly confessed his allegiance to the Lord Jesus (verse 8). He told them that it was in the power and the name of the Lord Jesus Christ that he had healed the lame beggar.

He told them that the Lord Jesus was raised from the dead and that he was the foundation stone on which salvation was built. He boldly stated that apart from the Lord Jesus, whom they had crucified, there was no salvation. In saying this he was telling them that they were lost and without hope. These were courageous words. This time Peter was filled with the Spirit of God. He was no longer ashamed. The Spirit of God had driven away all shame and fear.

Verse 13 tells us that the Jewish religious leaders were astonished at the boldness of Peter and John. Though they were uneducated and ordinary men, there was something different about them. The leaders noted that Peter and John had been with Jesus.

As much as this council wanted to deny what had taken place, they could not. Even these enemies noticed the difference in the lives of the apostles. They saw the Lord Jesus in them. Verse 14 tells us that the Jewish leaders were speechless before the apostles and the healed man. The evidence was undeniable.

The Jewish leaders wanted to discuss the situation privately so they sent the apostles away. The men of the Sanhedrin knew that they could not deny the miracle, and they had heard the apostles explain the source of their power. As they discussed the issue, their concern was to keep as many people as possible from becoming Christians (verse 17). The Jewish leaders were more concerned for their traditions than they were with the truth. They decided to warn the apostles against teaching any more about the Lord Jesus.

Peter was not threatened by what they said. He told them clearly that he would continue to preach what God had put on his heart (verses 19–20). He would not hold back. Peter experienced what the prophet Jeremiah felt when he tried to stop speaking in the name of the Lord: "But if I say, 'I will not mention him or speak any more in his name,' his word is in my heart like a fire, a fire shut up in my bones. I am weary of holding it in; indeed, I cannot" (Jeremiah 20:9).

The Spirit of God had compelled Peter to preach about the Lord. To refuse to speak about the Lord Jesus was not possible. Preaching in the name of the Lord Jesus was not an option or effort for Peter and the apostles. It was the natural result of a Spirit-filled life.

How often have we pushed ourselves to speak in the name of Jesus? How often have we had to force ourselves to spend time in prayer? It seems that our experience as Christians is one of constantly pushing ourselves to do God's will. Why do we wrestle so much with our Christian faith? Could it be because we have quenched the Holy Spirit?

As individuals filled with the Spirit of God, it is natural for us to enjoy the presence of God. Spending time with the Lord ought never to be a chore. The Spirit of God fills our hearts with a desire for God and his Word. He will lead us to passionately seek God. Under his direction and guidance, our souls are never satisfied with our present experience of God. We constantly hunger for more. Admittedly, we have not always allowed the Spirit of God to work this way in our lives. There have been times when we have grieved him and his work in us. If we allow him, however, the Spirit of God will fill us with a desire for God and move us to serve him boldly.

Why do we experience so much difficulty in our Christian walk? Is it not because we are trying to live the Christian faith in our own strength? We have been trying to gather up from our old nature a love and desire for God—it will never work. The old nature wants nothing to do with God. Do you want your experience to be like the apostles, who could not help speaking out for God? Probably the greatest thing you could ever do is to stop trying to find that strength in yourself. The willingness and the power to live the Christian life are not in us. Only when the Spirit of God moves in us will we find great delight and power in doing the will of God.

Having threatened the apostles, the leaders sent them away without punishment because they were afraid of the people's reaction. What a contrast we have here in these verses between the Jewish leaders and the apostles. The Jewish leaders could not do anything for fear of what people would think. The apostles, on the other hand, cared nothing for what people thought. We can only feel sorry for the Jewish leaders. who were so trapped by their traditions and fear of people. I cannot help thinking that maybe someone who is reading this book might be in the very same situation. Maybe you cannot grow in your walk with God because you are trapped like these Jewish leaders. Maybe your traditions and the fear of what others might think have blinded you to the truth and kept you from growing in your walk with the Lord. May the Spirit of God break those chains today.

For Consideration:

- Do you experience boldness for the Lord? What holds you back?

- How much of your Christian life is lived in your own strength?

- Is it possible to live the Christian life in your own strength? How much of your struggle with the Christian life is because you are trying to do the Spirit's work yourself?

For Prayer:

- Confess your attempts to live the Christian life in your own strength.

- Ask the Lord to help you die to self and let the Spirit live the life of Christ through you.

- Ask him to give you the boldness of the apostles.

10

Renewed Strength

Read Acts 4:23–31

Peter and John had just been released from prison after a stern warning from the Sanhedrin (the Jewish ruling council). After their release they decided to meet with the church and share what had happened. There may have been a couple of reasons for visiting the church at this time.

First, the apostles knew that the church would be very concerned about them. The Lord had died at the hands of the Sanhedrin. We can be sure that much prayer had gone up for Peter and John during their stay in prison and their meeting with the council. The apostles wanted to reassure their friends that God had been faithful and answered their prayers. This would be a real encouragement to the church.

The second reason the apostles would have returned to the church would probably have been for their own personal encouragement. The apostles had been through a very trying time. They needed to regroup and reflect on what had happened. Being with their fellow believers would have built them up in their faith.

The apostles informed the church about what the chief priests and elders had said to them and how they had been commanded not to speak or teach in the name of the Lord Jesus (verse 23). The church would have been concerned about this reaction on the part of the Jewish leaders. The apostles knew what could happen to them if they disregarded the warning.

We can only imagine what the tone of this meeting would have been. The church as a whole had been going through a high point in its experience. These disciples lived together and shared all their resources. They saw the working of the Spirit of God in their midst. In just a short while, they had grown from one hundred and twenty members to over five thousand. Each new believer had all the excitement that comes with a new faith in the Lord. These were exciting times. Now these believers had to face the realization that there was going to be strong opposition to their faith. Things were not going to be easy for them. How would the realization that they risked losing their lives affect their morale?

This whole situation drove these believers to their knees in prayer. Notice how they addressed God. They came to him as the sovereign God (verse 24). What is God's sovereignty? It is that characteristic of God that gives him absolute right, absolute authority, and absolute control over all of his creation. These believers approached a God who had absolute control of the situation in which they found themselves. He was the God who made the heavens and the earth and everything in them. Would a few Jewish leaders be able to defeat them if the creator of the universe was on their side?

The whole thought process was so simple. If God was on their side, what did they have to worry about? Would the creator of the universe not have the strength or wisdom to care for them in this situation? It seems so simple and yet we often miss the point. How often have we, in much less threatening situations, worried ourselves sick? We have to admire the simple faith of these early followers of Christ.

As the believers prayed, they were reminded of the words of David in Psalm 2:1–2. Here David lamented the fact that the nations and the rulers of his day opposed the things of God. They raged, plotted, and took their vain stand against the Lord. Nothing had changed by the time of the apostles. The early church experienced what David had experienced from God's enemies. The church formed in a day when secular and religious officials did not respect the things of God. These disciples lived in an age when their leaders openly turned their backs on the Lord Jesus and his Word. They had seen Pontius Pilate and the people of Israel conspire against the Lord Jesus. These believers had seen God's enemies hang the Savior of the world on a cross and watch him die. The church understood the spiritual nature of the battle.

Notice the comfort the disciples took in the Lord's control (verse 28). They realized that the sovereign Lord who created the universe also controlled its destiny. All things were in his hands. This control extended even over the evil decisions of the people who had killed the Lord Jesus. God had used their bitterness and hatred to accomplish the salvation of his people. God used the death of the Lord Jesus, at the hands of evil men, to accomplish his purposes. God could turn evil into good. What a comfort this was for these believers in their situation. They refused to be discouraged. As long as God was sitting on the throne of the universe, there would be hope.

I do not know what your situation might be, but I know that there is comfort in bowing before the sovereign God.

Nothing is too hard for him. He will work out all things for his glory and your good. There is no reason to lose heart.

After recognizing the sovereignty of God in their situation, the believers petitioned him for strength (verse 29). Notice that they did not pray that God would change their situation. They accepted it as having come from a sovereign God. Instead, they prayed for boldness to face the opposition.

There is a very important lesson in this. As Christians, we have a tendency to pray for the removal of our problems and not for boldness to face them. I fear that our persistence in asking God to remove these obstacles may be our downfall. God sends us trials for our own good. A quick examination of the early church shows that tribulation brought new growth and vitality to the body of Christ. It is only in accepting what a sovereign God sends our way that we can experience the growth and vitality that these things are meant to accomplish. These first-century disciples submitted to the care of a sovereign God. Though they did not understand the reason behind their trials, they accepted them as from the Lord and committed themselves to learning what God wanted them to learn.

The disciples petitioned God not only for boldness to continue preaching the Word but also for the power to demonstrate the reality of Christ through miracles and wonders (verse 30). They had just seen how the healing of the lame beggar had caused many men and women to turn to the Savior. They were not looking for power for themselves. They craved the reality of a living Christ in their midst. They wanted others to know that the Lord Jesus had risen from the dead. They wanted to see a powerful working of the Spirit of God. They wanted the gifts of the Spirit to be manifested.

It does not take much to satisfy us. Where are those who crave a real moving of the Spirit of God in our midst?

Where are those who so seek the reality of God that they will petition him as did the early church?

God did not delay in answering this prayer of the early church. When these disciples had finished praying, the Spirit of God fell afresh on them. They were filled with the boldness they had asked for. In the midst of their trial, they experienced the great blessing of God.

What trial are you facing today? The boldness and strength he gave to these early Christians can be yours as well. Won't you accept the trials he has sent your way and let him teach you what he wants through them? God will not fail to meet you in your trial.

For Consideration:

- Are you facing a particular trial today? What comfort do you take from the fact that God is a sovereign God?

- Consider some of the trials that you have gone through in life. How has God used those trials to shape you more into his image?

For Prayer:

- Take time to thank the Lord that he is sovereign in your trial today. Ask him for boldness to directly face that trial.

- Thank him for what he will accomplish through that trial in your life.

- Do you know someone else facing a trial today? Pray for God's blessing on them in their trial.

- The early church cried out for a deeper manifestation of the presence of the Spirit and power of the Lord. Ask God to use you in a deeper way to be a demonstration of his character and power.

11

Ananias and Sapphira

Read Acts 4:32–5:11

You can be sure that when the Spirit of God is at work, so is the enemy. The story of Ananias and Sapphira reminds us that even the early church had problems.

Acts 4:32–37 gives us the background to the story of Ananias and Sapphira. The evidence of the Spirit's presence in the lives of the early believers is seen in their love and practical care for one another. Verse 32 tells us that the church was of one heart and mind. What does it mean to be of one heart and mind? This passage gives us the answer. Church members shared everything they had. Land, houses, and possessions were being sold and the money donated to the church. This money was distributed to the brothers and sisters who had particular needs. We see an example of this in the case of Barnabas in verses 36–37.

When the Holy Spirit came to the believers, he caused them to reorganize their priorities in life. Some of these individuals had amassed wealth. Having these possessions usually meant increased respect and influence in the community. When the Spirit of God came on them, however, something happened. Priorities were radically shifted. They no longer lived for the moment. The accumulation of physical wealth lost its attraction when compared to knowing Christ. So deep was their experience of Christ, that the pleasure of accumulating possessions lost its appeal. Beyond this, however, was the fact that the Spirit of Christ was changing their orientation. Before this, they had been self-oriented. In other words, life had revolved around personal needs. Their thoughts had been for their own comfort and enjoyment. When the Spirit of God came to them, they became more like Christ. Their orientation changed from being self-oriented to being "others-oriented." The Spirit of God opened their eyes to the needs of those around them. The love of Christ in their hearts constrained them to sacrifice their own interests for the well-being of their brothers and sisters. The result of this was that the needy people were ministered to.

Not only were physical needs being met but so were spiritual needs. In verse 33 we discover that the apostles continued to preach the resurrection of Christ with great power. God's grace (unmerited favor) was on them as they ministered. Often we think of the ministry of the Spirit of God as being uniquely spiritual in nature, but here we see him leading individuals to minister to the physical needs of the people. The early church, led by the Spirit, ministered to both spiritual and physical needs. This was the heart of Jesus in his ministry on earth. He ministered to the whole person, both physically and spiritually.

It is in this context that we meet a couple named Ananias and Sapphira (5:1). The ministry of the early church had touched Ananias and Sapphira. They had seen the moving of the Spirit of God in the lives of church members. This couple watched as believers sold their houses and land and brought the money to the apostles for distribution among the poor. All this so deeply touched the lives of Ananias and Sapphira that they decided to sell a piece of property and give the money to the apostles for distribution. The problem, however, was that they were not sure that they really wanted to give the full value of the property. As they discussed this issue between themselves, they decided that they would sell the property, keep a portion for themselves, and give the rest to the apostles saying that they had given the full amount.

When this couple brought the money to the apostles, the Lord revealed to Peter that Ananias was lying to the Holy Spirit by keeping a portion for himself (verse 3). When Peter confronted him about this, Ananias fell to the ground dead. A young man wrapped up his body and buried him. Three hours later, Sapphira arrived. Peter asked her if the amount her husband had brought in earlier was the amount they had received for the land. She lied to Peter by telling him that it was. With that, she too was struck dead. The young man who had buried her husband returned to bury her.

What was the sin of Ananias and Sapphira? Is it that they kept a portion of the money for themselves? This does not seem to be the case. In verse 4, Peter recognized that the property rightly belonged to Ananias. Even after the sale of the property, the money was at his disposal. Peter told him that he could have done what he wanted with the money. This would lead us to understand that it would have been completely acceptable for Ananias and Sapphira to offer a portion of the proceeds from the sale of their property to the church and keep the rest. What was the sin that merited death?

Verse 3 tells us that Satan was behind the sin of Ananias and Sapphira. Satan had already used the Sanhedrin in his attempt to discourage the church in its progress. The threats of the Sanhedrin, however, had not discouraged the church. Satan needed to find another way of stopping the work of the Spirit. According to Peter, Satan filled the heart of Ananias and caused him to lie to the Holy Spirit. Ananias and Sapphira yielded themselves to Satan and his prompting. They had become his instruments to attack the work of the Spirit of God in the life of the early church. Satan knew that if he could infiltrate the church with just one couple who would live a lie, then he would be able to grieve the Spirit of God and slow down the progress of the gospel. God revealed this to Peter so that it could be immediately dealt with.

In what way did the couple lie to the Holy Spirit? It is obvious from verses 4 and 8 that both Ananias and Sapphira had attempted to deceive the church into thinking that they had given everything, when in reality they had kept a portion for themselves. As we have already said, their sin was not in the fact that they kept some of the money for themselves. Their sin was twofold: they listened to Satan, and they lied to the church. In these things they were guilty before God. Their action could be compared to the sin of Achan in Joshua 7, who hid what he had stolen from the city of Jericho in his tent. God had refused to give Israel victory over the people of Ai because of the hidden sin of Achan. Ananias and Sapphira boldly lied to the church in the presence of the Holy Spirit. In so doing, they were guilty of blasphemy.

By lying to the Holy Spirit and the apostles, Ananias and Sapphira were giving Satan a foothold in the church. The work of God progresses as people recognize their sin and turn their hearts over to God. The Spirit of God was moving in the lives of his people in those days. If Ananias and Sapphira had had their way, the blessing of the Lord would have been removed from the church, even as it was in the days of Achan. Like Judas, Satan filled the hearts of Ananias and Sapphira. He sent them as his ambassadors to sow seeds of sin in the midst of the thriving early church. Peter recognized the action of Ananias and Sapphira as a satanic attack on the work of God. Like Judas, this couple had willingly consented to being Satan's instruments. They had willingly consented to infiltrate the church with deceit and lies. This had to be taken seriously. The situation had to be dealt with immediately, before it destroyed what God was doing in their midst.

What does all this have to teach us today? Does this passage not challenge us about the need of being vigilant? Satan is the master of deceit. In this passage, he sent a couple to the church with a large gift for the work of God. This very gift would have been the downfall of the church. Satan can infiltrate the work of God by means of good and proper activities. How we need the discernment of Peter. I wonder how many ministries Satan has similarly infiltrated today? Our enemy knows our practical needs. He will not hesitate to send us a neatly wrapped answer to those needs if by so doing he can distract us from the work at hand. May God give us discernment to recognize this when it comes our way.

For Consideration:

- Consider for a moment the reorganization of priorities and the shift of orientation in the life of the early church. Do we see this in churches today?

- Is it possible that the sin of Ananias and Sapphira is being repeated in our day? What wrongly motivates people to contribute to the work of God?

- How do we recognize and deal with people like Ananias and Sapphira in our churches?

For Prayer:

- Ask the Lord to give you his mind with regard to his priorities for your life.

- Pray for your spiritual leaders that they would have the discernment of Peter in dealing with people like Ananias and Sapphira.

- Thank God that even though the enemy is active, we are more than overcomers in Christ.

12

Holy Boldness

Read Acts 5:12–42

Peter and John had just been released from prison (see chapter 4). The Sanhedrin, which imprisoned them, gave them a stern warning. They were not to preach anymore in the name of Jesus. This warning needed to be taken seriously, for it was this very council that had prosecuted Jesus and sent him to Pilate for crucifixion. This warning, to most people, would have been enough. The simple understanding that they could lose their lives if they disregarded the wishes of this council could have caused them to retreat into silence. However, this was not the response of the apostles. They had a ministry to accomplish. The Jewish ruling council would not hinder them. They chose to risk death and persecution rather than turn their backs on the ministry the Lord had given them.

The prayer of the church in chapter 4 had been twofold. These disciples had prayed for an increase in evidence of the ministry of the Holy Spirit in their midst, and they had prayed for boldness to face the opposition that was coming their way. Both of these prayers were answered.

Greater evidence of the ministry of the Holy Spirit

While some Jews feared being associated with the followers of Christ because of the Sanhedrin, there was very clear evidence of the work of God in the church. How else could the unity and growth in number be explained? An outsider could see in the church a true demonstration of the love of Christ in action. Though not accepted by the Jewish leaders, these early believers were greatly respected in the community. God was among them in power. The result of this was that more and more people believed in the Lord.

Verse 12 tells us that the apostles performed many miracles and signs. This was exactly what the church had prayed for: "Stretch out your hand to heal and perform miraculous signs and wonders through the name of your holy servant Jesus" (4:30). Men and women brought their sick into the streets and laid them on beds and mats with the hope that as Peter passed by, his shadow would perhaps heal them. (There is no indication in this passage that Peter's shadow healed anyone, but it does give us an understanding of what the crowds were thinking.) The sick and those possessed with evil spirits were brought to the apostles, and all of them were being delivered and healed. The presence of the Spirit of God was very clear at this time. Obviously God had answered believers' prayers that signs and wonders would be done in their midst.

Boldness to face the opposition

The other request of the disciples was for boldness to speak the Word in the face of opposition that came their way. We see the Lord's answer to this request very clearly in this chapter. These believers continued to meet in the temple (verse 12). It would have been quite possible for them to go into hiding, but they had no desire to do so. They had a message to proclaim, and many people needed to hear the truth. They courageously continued to meet and preach the good news of the kingdom. The result was that many people came to know the Lord (verse 14).

This holy boldness led to the arrest of the apostles. Verse 17 tells us that the Sadducees were jealous. They could not bear to see the crowds desert them to follow the apostles. The Sanhedrin cast the apostles into prison to await trial. During the night an angel of the Lord came to them in their prison cell, opened the doors of the cell, and brought them out of the prison, without waking the guards. Having given the apostles their freedom, the angel commanded them to return to the temple and preach the message of new life in Christ.

What would your response have been to the angel? These apostles were in prison for preaching the gospel. It would be understandable to leave the city of Jerusalem and preach somewhere else, far away from the opposition, but to return to the temple where they were first arrested was quite another matter. To return to the temple was to risk even more vengeance on the part of the religious leaders. At daybreak, however, the apostles were at the temple, preaching the good new of Jesus. Where did they get this boldness? Was it not the result of the prayer of the church: "Now, Lord, consider their threats and enable your servants to speak your word with great boldness" (4:29). There can be no doubt that the Lord answered this prayer as well.

When the Sanhedrin convened in the morning, they sent to the jail for the apostles. When the officers returned with the news that the apostles were not there, the men of the council were puzzled. What was even more perplexing was that everything was locked and the guards were standing at their places. There was no possible way these men could have escaped. Even as the leaders were trying to figure this out, someone came with the news that the apostles were in the temple, teaching the people. Guards were immediately dispatched to bring them before the council. The guards used no force because they were afraid of the reaction of the people.

The Sanhedrin reminded the apostles of the warning not to teach any more in the name of Jesus. Peter bluntly stated that they had to obey God rather than men (verse 29). In other words, the apostles had no intention of listening to the Sanhedrin. Peter also told them that they were guilty of killing the Son of God by hanging him on a tree as a common criminal. Peter told them, in no uncertain terms, that though they had killed Jesus, God had raised him from the dead and made him to be Prince and Savior. Jesus was seated at the right hand of God. The apostles were "witnesses to these things," as was the Holy Spirit who dwelt in them (verse 32). Again, we see the evidence of holy boldness in the lives of the apostles. They did not shrink from their accusers.

The response of the council was very predictable. They were furious. They wanted to put the apostles to death. This holy boldness led to much opposition. Notice, however, that the Lord who filled the apostles with boldness also surrounded them with his protecting hand. A Pharisee named Gamaliel stood up in the Sanhedrin. Verse 34 tells us that he was very well respected and honored by the people of his day. He asked that the apostles be removed from the room while he addressed the council.

Gamaliel cautioned the council about their intentions of killing the apostles. He reminded them of similar situations in their recent history. He related the story of two Jewish revolutionaries. The first was a man named Theudas who came with great claims about himself and his abilities. He gained a following of four hundred men. He ended up being killed, his followers were dispersed, and the whole thing came to nothing. The second man was Judas the Galilean.

He led a band of followers in political revolt. He too was killed and his followers scattered. His efforts also came to nothing.

Gamaliel's advice to the council was that they leave the apostles alone. There was something different about this movement. This movement was similar to these other movements in that it too had a leader, a large following, and the leader had been killed. What was different, however, was that the death of their leader had not weakened their zeal. In fact, this movement was growing in number and influence in Jerusalem. There were things that were taking place in this movement that could not be explained. Gamaliel was afraid that if this movement was of God, they would be wrong to kill the apostles. He felt it wise to leave the whole matter in the hands of God. He believed that if the movement was not of God, it would come to nothing, even as the other movements he mentioned.

Gamaliel's speech persuaded the Sanhedrin not to kill the apostles. Instead, the council had the apostles flogged and then ordered them not to preach in the name of the Lord Jesus (verse 40). God had again been faithful to the apostles. They left the Sanhedrin that day rejoicing in the goodness of God. They rejoiced in the fact that they were worthy to suffer in the name of the Lord Jesus. It was a privilege for them to stand up for their Lord. The joy of the Holy Spirit was poured out abundantly on them that day. In the midst of their trials, they knew joy beyond measure. It was as though the smile of God's approval was on them because of their faithfulness. They had not grieved the Holy Spirit by disobedience or fear.

Though they had been warned a second time not to speak in the name of the Lord Jesus, the apostles met every day in the temple court and in homes in Jerusalem, teaching that Jesus was the Christ. Nothing would stop them from boldly proclaiming the gospel of their Lord. Had the twofold prayer of the church in Acts 4:29–30 been answered? There can be no doubt that God had answered this prayer. The work of the Spirit of God was much in evidence. The boldness of the apostles was a result of his work in their lives.

Do we experience this holy boldness in our lives? We will never find this boldness in ourselves. This boldness comes from the Spirit of God alone. It is not natural to our human nature. It can only be ours as we die to ourselves and allow the Spirit of God to fill our hearts and lives. Where the Spirit of God reigns, there will be boldness for the Lord. There will also be powerful evidence of his presence. May this be our experience.

For Consideration:

• Have you ever found yourself ashamed of the gospel? What keeps you from speaking out with boldness?

• What is the difference between boldness and being obnoxious?

• What evidence is there of the presence of the Holy Spirit in your life?

For Prayer:

• Ask forgiveness for the times when you have been ashamed of the gospel.

• Ask the Lord to give you that boldness for him and his Word.

• Ask the Lord to use you by his Holy Spirit to be an instrument of his power in this dying world.

13

The First Deacons

Read Acts 6:1–7

As we study the book of Acts, there are two parallel themes that keep coming to the surface. The first theme relates to the powerful working of the Spirit of God in the lives of his people. The second is the constant attack of the enemy on the church. We have seen, to this point, how the enemy has sought to discourage the church by using the Sanhedrin to threaten and imprison the apostles. This caused the church instead to ask for more boldness. Satan then tried to infiltrate the church by means of deception through Ananias and Sapphira. Peter recognized this deception right away and God struck the couple dead before they could do any damage to the church. In this passage we will see a third attempt on the part of Satan to destroy the work of the church.

The work of God was progressing rapidly in Jerusalem. Verse 1 tells us that the number of disciples was continually increasing. More and more individuals were coming to know the Lord Jesus as Savior. This rapid growth put a strain on the leaders of the church. With the increase in number (now well over five thousand people) came an increase in the work of food distribution to the needy. Here was an open door for Satan to disrupt the work of the Spirit.

The increased workload meant that the apostles had to concentrate a certain amount of time to help in this practical matter of the distribution of food. While this was a very important ministry, it took the apostles away from their primary calling of preaching the Word. By filling their time with other good activities, Satan could distract the apostles from the task to which God had called them. How often has Satan used this technique in our day? How many pastors have become so active in the many activities of their churches that they no longer have time to use and develop the gifts God has given them? Do not be surprised if Satan fills your schedule with good and necessary things to distract you from your real calling.

Notice here that the apostles refused to get caught in this trap. In verse 2 they reminded the church that it would not be right for them to leave the ministry of the Word to serve tables. They were not saying that serving tables was beneath their dignity. What they were saying was that God had given them a particular calling. God had gifted them in the ministry of preaching the Word. They were accountable to God for the use of these gifts. It would be wrong for them to become sidetracked into another ministry.

This principle is so important for us today. There is no end to the opportunities we have to serve the Lord. We simply do not have enough resources, gifts, and strength to meet the needs of everyone who comes our way. How often have we seen individuals who have stretched themselves so thin that they can no longer do a good job in anything? How Satan must delight in his accomplishments in the lives of these people. He has made them useless to the kingdom of

God. How we need people who understand God's call on their lives. Men and women who refuse to be sidetracked from the ministry to which God has called them know when to say no, for the sake of the kingdom of God.

Notice that not only did Satan seek to hinder the work by distracting the apostles but he also sought to create division in the church. The first church members were of two sorts. There were the Hebraic Jews and the Grecian Jews. It is not completely understood today what the difference was between these Jews. It may be that the difference was geographical. The Hebraic Jews would have been those who were born in Israel, while the Grecian Jews were born outside of Israel. The problem with this distinction, however, is the fact that Paul was from Tarsus (outside Israel) and he considered himself a Jew of Jews. He was as Jewish as any Jew born in Israel. It may also have been that the difference was one of language and culture. There would have been many Jews at this point in history who did not speak Hebrew. While they observed the traditions of the fathers to some extent, they had not maintained their language. They were influenced by Greek culture and language.

It would appear from history that these Grecian Jews were not considered on the same level as the Hebraic Jews. Hebraic Jews saw themselves as pure Jews. They had resisted the influence of hated foreign cultures. They had maintained the language and culture of Abraham, Isaac, and Jacob. To them, the Grecian Jews were in a lower class. Satan, knowing the tension that existed between these two groups, decided to use it for his own advantage. It appears that the Hebraic Jews were catering to their own kind. The Grecian Jews were being neglected in the daily distribution of food.

It is important that we clean up all the baggage of our past sinful lives. How often have our pasts come back to haunt us as Christians? We discover that the early church needed to be cleansed of prejudices and pride. In Christ all believers were made one. There were no longer to be social distinctions such as Hebraic Jews and Grecian Jews, but these people still clung to old prejudices. Satan, knowing this weakness, decided to use it to infiltrate the church with dissension and infighting. Satan would love to do the same to the church today. Indeed, in many cases he has succeeded in pitting Christian against Christian. Doctrinal issues, issues related to Christian liberty, issues related to the traditions of our churches, and personal preferences tend to divide us as believers. Our enemy knows that if he can keep us fighting among ourselves, we will be of no use whatsoever to God and the work of reaching this world will never be realized. The blessing of God will be removed from us. Ultimately, we will become useless to God and his kingdom. Satan's tactics have not changed over the years. Why should he change his tactics when the church keeps falling into the same old traps?

The apostles knew that something needed to be done to solve this problem. They could not let Satan get the upper hand. Realizing that the ministry of distributing food would take them away from their calling, the apostles recommended that the church choose seven men from their midst to take on this responsibility. These men would become the first deacons of the early church. Their role was one of practical service to the church.

Notice that while these men would serve the church in practical matters, they were nonetheless required to be spiritual men. These candidates needed to be filled with the Holy Spirit. How could the church know if an individual was filled with the Holy Spirit? To this point in our study of the book of Acts, we have seen several indications of this.

First, Jesus told his disciples in Acts 1:8 that when the Holy Spirit came on them, they would be his witnesses. This is test number one. Do you want to know if a person is filled with the Holy Spirit? Ask yourself what kind of witness the person is for the Lord Jesus. Does this person's life stand out in a crowd as being a testimony to the Lord Jesus?

Second, we see in the book of Acts that when the Holy Spirit came to the church, priorities were radically changed. Those filled with the Holy Spirit shifted from being self-centered to being others-centered. They experienced an unnatural love in their hearts for their brothers and sisters in Christ. They were willing to sell all they had for the sake of a brother in need. They were no longer interested in the amassing of great wealth for themselves. Do you want to know if a person is filled with the Holy Spirit? Examine how this person deals with brothers and sisters in Christ. Watch the person's use of resources. Is there a concern for others? Is the love of Christ evident?

Third, we notice in the book of Acts that those who were filled with the Holy Spirit stepped out boldly in the name of the Lord Jesus. In the last meditation we saw that the apostles were not afraid of what people might do to them or say to them. They stood up for the name of the Lord Jesus and risked their lives for him. They were more concerned about obedience to the call of Christ than they were for their own reputations. If their obedience meant dying for the Lord, then they were willing to accept it. Do you want to know if a person is filled with the Holy Spirit? Ask yourself if this person is willing to risk everything to be obedient to the Lord Jesus. Is this person willing to leave everything behind for the sake of Christ and sacrifice pride and reputation to be more obedient?

When the apostles asked the church to choose men who were known to be filled with the Spirit of God, they were in reality asking the church to choose men who had shown the above qualities in their lives. Notice that the church did not look for men who *might* in time show these characteristics. These qualities had to be already in place in their lives.

The deacon had to be an individual who not only was known to be filled with the Holy Spirit but also full of wisdom. There is a difference between wisdom and knowledge. Knowledge relates to information. Wisdom relates to the application of that knowledge to real life. What was the role of these deacons? Was it not in dealing with the practical, down-to-earth matters of the early church? Does it not follow that these men would need not only to be knowledgeable of the truth but also able to apply this truth to the practical issues of church life? While the apostles focused on the spiritual ministry of the Word, the deacons would move the church ahead in the practical application of that Word in the daily routine of the church.

Seven men were chosen. These men were ordained to their ministry by the laying on of hands by the apostles. The result was that the Word of God spread. God's work continued, in spite of the efforts of Satan to stop it. A large number of priests, in particular, came to know the Lord.

The efforts of Satan were stopped because God's people sought God's will first in their church life. The apostles refused to be sidetracked from their God-given calling. They immediately addressed the grievance of the Grecian Jews. They could have chosen to avoid such a controversial issue, but they refused to allow old prejudices to hinder them in their responsibility before God. Satan was powerless before such a church.

For Consideration:

- What gifts has the Lord given you? How are you using them for his glory? What things tend to distract you from the use of your gifts?

- What type of things can divide Christians today? How do we deal with these differences in the church?

- What were the qualifications of those who served in the role of deacon in the early church? Are you a spiritual leader? Do you have these qualifications?

For Prayer:

- Ask the Lord to help your church deal with differences existing among members.

- Pray for the spiritual leadership within your church. Ask the Lord for wisdom for them in dealing with the various issues of church life.

- Ask the Lord to give you a spiritual leadership that demonstrates the qualifications outlined in this chapter.

14

Stephen

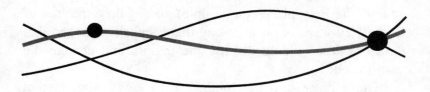

Read Acts 6:8–8:3

We have seen at least three efforts of Satan to destroy the work of the Spirit of God in the early church. In chapter 4 Satan sought to discourage the church by the threats of the Sanhedrin. When this did not work, he sought to infiltrate the church with the deceit and lies of Ananias and Sapphira. Again, his efforts were thwarted. In the beginning part of this chapter, we see how a dispute between the Hebraic and the Grecian Jews could have been disastrous to the life of this early church. When these efforts were not successful, Satan moved to measures that were more drastic. In this chapter we will see how he resorted to blatant lies and open persecution.

Stephen was one of the seven deacons chosen by the early church. He was a man who showed evidence of the power of God in his life. God was doing many miraculous signs in the life of this man. Verse 10 indicates that Stephen also had a powerful preaching ministry that stirred up a certain group of Jews in Jerusalem. The Synagogue of the Freedmen (Libertines, KJV) took exception to what Stephen was preaching. These men challenged Stephen, but they could not stand up to the wisdom of the Holy Spirit in him. Because they could get nowhere in debate with Stephen, they decided to change their tactics. They secretly persuaded some men to say that Stephen had blasphemed Moses and God. None of these accusations were true. The result, however, was that Stephen was brought before the Sanhedrin. The false witnesses claimed that Stephen continuously spoke against the holy place (the temple) and against the law of God. They went as far as to say that Stephen preached that the Lord Jesus would destroy the temple and change the traditions of Moses.

Those present in the Sanhedrin that day noticed that something was happening to Stephen as these lies were being spread about him—his face was like the face of an angel (6:15). While I have never seen an angel, I think that what these people saw that day was a glow of joy and peace. Maybe they saw something of what the people of Israel saw when Moses returned from the top of the mountain with his face glowing with the glory of God (Exodus 34:29–30). What is evident from this is that Stephen was not in the least concerned with what was taking place. He was wrapped up in the presence of God. God's peace and joy filled his heart. Maybe God was letting him know that very soon he would be in heaven. Maybe Stephen saw the Lord Jesus himself calling him to his side. I have often heard people say that they did not feel that they could ever have the courage to stand up for the Lord as the martyrs of old. In his moment of need, however, Stephen was empowered to do what God had called him to do. He would shortly lay down his life. He did not hesitate to do this because the Spirit of God had filled him with the joy of the Lord. In the Spirit of God, he was strong.

When Stephen was asked if the charges against him were true, he chose not to answer. He was not interested in defending himself. Could it be that he knew his end had come? Stephen instead chose to preach the gospel. Let's examine what he told the Sanhedrin.

Stephen began by speaking about Abraham (7:2–8). He reminded his audience that God had called their forefather from Haran to go to a land that he would show him. Abraham left his homeland in obedience to the call of God. God promised him the land of Canaan (later renamed Israel) for his descendants. Abraham did not see the fulfillment of this promise himself, but God was faithful to his word. God entered into a covenant agreement with Abraham and his descendants, promising to be their God and they were to be his people.

During the time of Jacob, Joseph was sold into slavery in Egypt because of the jealousy of his brothers, the patriarchs (7:9). God did not abandon Joseph in his trial but proved faithful and caused Joseph to gain the good will of the Pharaoh of Egypt. Joseph became the second in command of the nation of Egypt. At this time a severe famine struck Canaan and God used Joseph to protect his people. There in Egypt, under the leadership of Joseph, God's covenant people were well cared for. God had again proved himself faithful to his people.

In the land of Egypt, God's people grew steadily in number. This provoked the jealousy of the new Pharaoh of Egypt. He oppressed the covenant people and treated them cruelly. Newborn male children were thrown into the river to drown. Again, God proved faithful to his people. He placed his hand on a young infant named Moses (7:20). Moses was raised by the daughter of Pharaoh. He became a very powerful individual in the land of Egypt, educated in all the wisdom of the land. When Moses was forty years old, he saw an Egyptian mistreating an Israelite. God used this incident to draw Moses into his mission. God took Moses into the desert of Midian and for forty years prepared him for his calling. When the time was right, God spoke to Moses in a burning bush and told him to return to the land of Egypt. Through this man, God delivered his people from their cruel oppressors. Again, God was faithful to his covenant relationship with his people.

In the desert God revealed his law to Moses. It was there that God organized his people into a great nation. There in the desert God gave them the tabernacle and instructed them in his holy ways.

As for God's people, however, they turned their backs on God in spite of all he had done for them. There in the desert they bowed down to the golden calf, fashioned by Moses' brother, Aaron. Stephen's sermon tells us that God's children bowed down in worship to the heavenly bodies (the stars, the sun, and the moon) and to the foreign gods of Molech and Rephan (7:42–43).

In spite of these sins in the desert, however, the Lord their God remained faithful to them. Under the reigns of David and Solomon, God's people reached their height of power and wealth. The temple that Solomon built was a massive and beautiful structure. It was not meant to house God, for as Isaiah wrote, God could not be confined to a physical building made by human hands (7:49–50). This temple was a sign of God's great covenantal blessings on his people, but God was greater than the temple.

In the times of the prophets, God sent one prophet after another to warn his people to turn from their sins, but they refused to listen. As Stephen said: "Was there ever a prophet your fathers did not persecute? They even killed those who predicted the coming of the Righteous One. And now you have betrayed and murdered him" (7:52).

What does all of this tell us about the people of God? God had been so very faithful to them. They, however, wanted nothing to do with God. God's people had a long history of turning their backs on the laws that Moses had given them and on the prophets that God had sent them. The people of Israel wanted to live their own lives and do things their own way. They did not love God. They had no desire to be faithful to the covenant.

Stephen's speech was powerful. He did not defend himself against the accusations of his false accusers. He simply reminded them of their own history recorded in the Word of God and spoke with holy boldness. He did not fear losing his life.

The response of the Sanhedrin was predictable. They "were furious and gnashed their teeth at him" (7:54). Stephen looked up into heaven and saw the Lord Jesus standing at the right hand of God. Stephen told them what he saw in his vision, but they blocked their ears. They did not want to hear what he had to say. They dragged him out of the city and stoned him. Even as they stoned him, the love of God poured out of him as the blood in his veins. "Lord, do not hold this sin against them" was his last request (7:60). With those words, he died. Not even in death would he hold a bitter thought against his accusers. Though Satan had been successful in killing this servant of God, Satan lost the battle. Stephen went to his master as a victorious saint. Satan had dealt a harsh blow, but Stephen resisted to the end. Again, the efforts of Satan were thwarted. God had shown himself to be more powerful than Satan.

One of the men present that day was a man named Saul, who later became known as the apostle Paul (8:1). He would prove initially to be one of the greatest enemies of this early church. From that day onward a great persecution broke out in the land. Saul would go from house to house, dragging believers off to prison. The church was forced to break up and scatter to avoid persecution. This, however, would only serve to spread of the good news to the rest of the world. In all of this, God was proving true to his promises.

For Consideration:

- What does this chapter teach us about God's patience with his people?

- Consider Stephen's willingness to forgive those who killed him. Do you have anything against a brother or sister? What do you need to do to make this right?

- What encouragement do you take from the example of Stephen?

- Can there be victory even in death?

For Prayer:

- Ask the Lord to help you endure to the end like Stephen.

- Ask him to heal your relationships with your brothers and sisters in Christ.

- Ask the Lord to give you some of the boldness of Stephen.

- Thank the Lord that he is victorious over sin and Satan.

15

Simon and the Samaritans

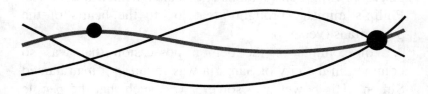

Read Acts 8:4–25

Persecution had broken out in Jerusalem. The church was scattered. While, to all appearances, this seemed to have been a tragic event, it did have its positive side. God used the scattered believers to spread the message of salvation beyond the walls of the city of Jerusalem. These believers proclaimed Christ wherever they went.

We met Stephen in the last two chapters. We now meet a second deacon of the early church named Philip. Like Stephen, Philip too was filled with the power of the Holy Spirit. Because of the persecution in Jerusalem, Philip went to the region of Samaria. There he began to preach the message of salvation. In those days, the Jews hated the Samaritans. Philip would have been very much aware of this animosity, but this did not hinder him from preaching the message of salvation in Samaria.

Samaria was not an easy place to minister. Many people were possessed by demons. Others suffered from physical afflictions. When the Samaritans heard Philip preach, however, and saw the miraculous signs he performed, they paid close attention to him. They received him as a messenger of God. Philip demonstrated power over unclean spirits, casting them out of those who were oppressed. In the power of Jesus' name, Philip healed those who came to him. None of these things were natural to Philip but were all evidences of the power of the Spirit of God that was at work in him. The result of Philip's ministry was that many were delivered from their demons and healed of their infirmities. Philip's ministry brought great joy to the hearts of the Samaritans (verse 8).

An example of the demon possession that was so common in the city of Samaria was found in a man named Simon. His power as a sorcerer was such that the people were amazed at what he could do. Simon was a proud person and boasted about his powers in the demonic realm. He was highly regarded as far as sorcerers were concerned. People from all classes of Samaritan society paid attention to him. From verse 10 we are led to believe that the people of Samaria considered Simon to be a god. They saw his power as divine. They called him the "Great Power." He had a large group of followers because of his magical skills. This tells us something about the community of Samaria and its bondage.

Philip met Simon and his followers in the city of Samaria. Simon and his disciples were so touched by the preaching of Philip that they believed and were baptized as followers of the Lord Jesus Christ. Verse 13 tells us that Simon himself believed and was baptized in the name of the Lord Jesus. Simon was particularly interested in the powerful miracles he saw Philip doing. He followed Philip everywhere he went.

Word soon returned to Jerusalem that the Lord was doing a work among the Samaritans. Peter and John were sent to see what was taking place. When the apostles arrived, they noticed that the Holy Spirit had not yet come on these individuals. According to verse 16 they had only been baptized in the name of Jesus. This is a difficult verse to understand. It seems that what the verse is telling us is that while they had received a water baptism, they had not yet been baptized by the Holy Spirit. While they had believed in the Lord Jesus, they had not received the Holy Spirit. Like the disciples before Pentecost, they believed but were not empowered by the Holy Spirit. It was not until Peter and John placed their hands on these new believers that they received the Holy Spirit. How should we to understand what was happening here? Why had the Holy Spirit not been given to these believers?

Some believe that the answer lies in the fact that these men and women needed to have the apostles lay their hands on them before they could receive the Holy Spirit. However, when the Holy Spirit came at Pentecost, no one laid hands on the believers; yet they were all filled (2:4). Others think that there was something missing in the faith of the Samaritans that hindered them from receiving the Holy Spirit. There is, however, no proof for this in the passage. We have no record of the apostles seeking to straighten out any lack in the faith of the Samaritans. It is indeed strange that, while Philip was himself filled with the Holy Spirit, able to cast out demons, and heal the sick, he was not able to pray that the Holy Spirit would fill these individuals who had recently come to faith.

This would lead us to assume that there must have been a very special reason why the blessing of the Holy Sprit was withheld from these Samaritan believers until the apostles could come to see them. We need to remember that the Jews hated the Samaritans. For many in the early church, salvation was for the Jews only. They could not possibly see how God could be interested in the Samaritans. Who would have believed that the Samaritans could equally receive the Holy

Spirit? God sent Peter and John, the foremost leaders of the early church, to Samaria to have them witness the coming of the Holy Spirit on another people group. What would have happened if the Holy Spirit had come to the Samaritans without Peter and John being there? Would the church in Jerusalem have accepted the Samaritans as brothers and sisters in Christ? It is quite likely that the Samaritans would still have been rejected. However, when the Samaritans received the Holy Spirit by means of the laying on of hands by Peter and John, the church had to realize that salvation was also for the Samaritans. Perhaps this was God's way of establishing unity in the church.

Simon was astonished to see how the Holy Spirit came on these Samaritans when the apostles laid hands on them. Simon wanted so desperately to have this power that he offered the apostles money for it. But Peter said: "May your money perish with you" (verse 20). Peter told Simon that he was captive to sin and that his heart was filled with bitterness. Simon could have no part in their ministry because he was not right with God. Peter used very bold words because he saw something quite evil in Simon.

Simon's desire was to control the Holy Spirit. He wanted to be able to use this power for himself. Simon was like a lot of us who want to be able to pray and immediately see God work. We want to see demons flee at our command. This attitude of seeking to control the power of God for our own end is sinful. It is not for us to control the power of God. It is rather for us to submit to that power and let it control us. God does what he wants, when he wants, and how he wants. Simon did not understand this.

Verse 13 tells us that Simon had believed and been baptized. However, from what Peter tells us, Simon had not really been saved from his sin. His acceptance of the message was based purely on what he saw Philip doing. Simon was attracted to the signs and wonders and wanted to be able to do them himself, though he had never yielded his heart to the Lord.

Peter leads us to believe that Simon and his money would perish because he thought he could buy the gift of the Holy Spirit. Simon needed to repent of his wickedness. What was so wicked about desiring to pay for the gift of the Spirit? First, it belittled the Spirit of God. Simon was treating the Holy Spirit as an object that could be bought or sold. In so doing, he showed great disrespect. Second, he wanted to use the Holy Spirit to promote himself. If he had this gift, people would certainly look up to him. The whole matter proved that Simon had not been changed. His heart was still the greedy and selfish heart it had always been. He only thought of himself and his own interests. It was for this reason that Peter told him that he needed to pray that the Lord would forgive him (verse 22). Simon then asked Peter to pray for him, but there is no evidence here to show that this man was truly repentant. He was concerned, however, about being judged.

When the apostles had finished their work in the region of Samaria, they returned to Jerusalem. On their way they preached in many Samaritan villages. They understood that the gospel was not only for Jews but for Samaritans as well. This had been clearly demonstrated to them in the way the Holy Spirit was working in that region.

For Consideration:

- What prejudices exist in the church today? Are there people we are not really reaching out to?

- What is it about Simon that shows us that he was not a true believer? Are there people like Simon in the church today?

- What evidence is there in your life that you have been empowered by the Holy Spirit, like the believers here in this chapter?

- Have you ever found yourself seeking to use the gifts that Lord has given you for your own glory? Why is this so wrong?

For Prayer:

- Thank the Lord that he does not have prejudices, as we have.

- Think of a group who has been ignored by the church today. Place them in the Lord's hands.

- Ask the Lord to open you up to the deeper empowering work of the Holy Spirit. Ask him to forgive you for seeking to do his work in your own strength.

16

The Ethiopian Eunuch

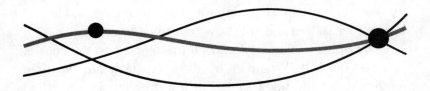

Read Acts 8:26–40

We saw in the last meditation how the gospel was first preached by the early church in the region of Samaria. This was in fulfillment of the promise of Jesus in Acts 1:8 where he told his disciples that when the Holy Spirit came on them, they would be his witnesses in Jerusalem, Judea, Samaria, and the uttermost parts of the earth. In this passage we will see how the gospel moved into Africa through the conversion of an Ethiopian.

Philip's ministry in the region of Samaria was being richly blessed of the Lord. The Holy Spirit had come on the Samaritans. Many had believed. Philip was in the midst of a revival. There was much work to be done.

It was in this context, however, that Philip heard the voice of an angel calling him to leave Samaria to follow the desert road that led from Jerusalem to Gaza. The distance from Samaria to Jerusalem was approximately forty miles (sixty kilometers). It was another fifty miles (eighty kilometers) from Jerusalem to Gaza. We have no record of Philip arguing with the angel about the wisdom of leaving these new converts. Philip left them in the hands of the Lord and set out in obedience to the word of the Lord. We also do not have any record of the angel explaining to Philip the reason for leaving the revival in Samaria. Philip had to move out in faith, not knowing what the Lord had in store for him.

As Philip traveled he met an Ethiopian eunuch who was a very important man in charge of the treasury of Candace, the queen of the Ethiopians. While this man was from Ethiopia, he was very open to learning the ways of the Jews. He had been in Jerusalem and was now returning home.

The Spirit of the Lord told Philip to go up to the chariot and stay with it. When Philip did this, he heard the man reading from the book of Isaiah the prophet. Philip asked the man if he understood what he was reading. The man responded: "How can I unless someone explains it to me" (verse 31). He invited Philip to come up into his chariot and sit with him.

The Ethiopian was reading from Isaiah 53:7–8. This passage speaks about the Lord Jesus and how he was led like a sheep to the slaughter, quietly accepted his destiny. The Lord of the universe was deprived of justice in his trial. He was killed, with no descendants to carry on his name. The Ethiopian did not know to whom the prophet was referring. He questioned Philip on this matter.

Notice how everything was perfectly orchestrated. Human effort could never have orchestrated such circumstances. How important it was for Philip to be in tune with the Spirit's leading. This whole event was Spirit-led from start to finish. Is this not the secret to reaching the world for Christ? How often have we tried to do things in our own strength and wisdom but failed? The ministry of Philip was successful because God was in it from start to finish.

The invitation of the Ethiopian to join him in his chariot

gave Philip an excellent opportunity to share the good news about the Lord Jesus. Obviously, what Philip said had a powerful impact on the Ethiopian. At that moment he gave his life to the Lord Jesus. When they came to some water along the side of the road, the Ethiopian asked Philip if he could immediately be baptized. His baptism was a symbol of his identification with the Lord Jesus whom he wanted to follow.

The King James Version (but not the NIV) records Philip telling the Ethiopian that if he believed with all his heart, he could be baptized. The eunuch then reassured Philip that he did believe that Jesus Christ was the Son of God (verse 37 KJV). The Ethiopian stopped the chariot, and he and Philip went down into the water. There in the desert Philip baptized this new believer.

When both men had come out of the water, the Bible tells us that the Spirit of God took Philip away and the eunuch did not see him again (verse 39). What actually happened to Philip? The Greek word indicates that the Holy Spirit seized Philip and took him away by force. There was no resistance on the part of Philip, and we are simply not told exactly how this took place. Did he simply disappear? Was he forcefully compelled by the Spirit to leave? There are passages in the Gospels stating that the Lord Jesus simply disappeared from the presence of his enemies when they pressed in to kill him (John 8:59; Luke 4:28–30). Perhaps this same sort of thing happened to Philip. The next thing we know about Philip is that he appeared in Azotus, some twenty miles (thirty-five kilometers) north of Gaza, where he continued to preach the gospel.

What does this passage have to do with us? We see from this passage that the ways of the Lord are very different from our ways. If it had been up to Philip, he might have stayed in Samaria, working with the new converts. This ministry would have been legitimate, but God had different plans.

Human wisdom is not always what it takes to advance the kingdom of God. It is more important for us to be in tune with God and his will. Our human strategies, as important as they are, must willingly submit to God's greater plan. Like Philip, we must be willing to drop everything and follow the Lord's leading.

Notice also the importance God places on the salvation of a single soul. Philip was affecting a whole community of believers in the region of Samaria. He was in the midst of a revival. However, God did not hesitate to take him from Samaria to share the good news with a single man on his way home from Jerusalem. At that precise moment, the Ethiopian eunuch was in need of someone to explain a passage of Scripture to him. Philip was the man sent to do it. God heard the cry of this one man. God knows the secrets of people's hearts. He heard the cry of the Ethiopian's heart. God knew he was ripe for the harvest. Philip would never have known this apart from the leading of the Spirit of God.

Maybe you say, "Who am I that God should be concerned with me?" Maybe you feel like the lonely Ethiopian on his way home from Jerusalem. A confused and lone voice cried out to God in the desert. God heard that cry and sent help. He will do the same for you. Each soul is precious to God.

Notice also in this passage that the Spirit of God overcame the social, cultural, and spiritual barriers between these two men. Although this Ethiopian was a high-ranking government official, he warmly received Philip into his chariot and opened his heart to what this total stranger had to say. This man was like a ripe fruit ready for the picking because God had been working in his heart before Philip's arrival. The circumstances were perfect. The result was guaranteed. All Philip did was share the Word and the Ethiopian accepted the Lord. How often have we wrestled to convince people of their need of the Lord? The Spirit of God broke through every obstacle in this encounter with the

Ethiopian. If God calls us to a work, we can be sure that he will also go before us to prepare the way.

When the work was finished, Philip was removed from the scene. He did not stay at the site to converse with the Ethiopian. There was other work to be done. God moved him on to his next responsibility. There were other souls to be won for the Lord. Philip's calling was to preach the good news. Others would build on the work he had begun. He was to move in obedience to the will of God. Like Philip, may we be able to distinguish God's voice and God's leading from the many other conflicting voices we hear all around us. It is only in obedience that we can expect real blessing.

For Consideration:

- From what we have seen in this meditation, why is it important that we be sensitive to the leading of the Holy Spirit in our lives and ministry?

- How can you tell the difference between your own ideas and the leading of the Holy Spirit?

- How many times do we get caught up in our own visions and agendas? How do we find the balance between using our God-given reasoning and listening for the Spirit's leading?

For Prayer:

- Thank the Lord that he knows what is best. Ask him to teach you to be sensitive to his leading.

- Thank him that he is concerned for those individuals who cry out to him from the desert places.

- Do you know of someone who is going through a desert place in life? Ask God to reach out to this person as he did to the Ethiopian.

17

The Conversion of Saul

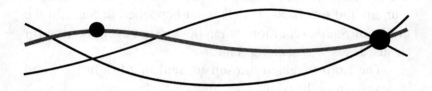

Read Acts 9:1–31

I n Acts 8 we read how the church of Jerusalem came under the heavy hand of persecution. When Stephen was martyred, the church scattered. One of the key figures in this persecution was a man named Saul.

Verse 1 tells us that Saul breathed out murderous threats against the church. The word "breathe" can also mean "to be bent on" or "to be animated by." These are powerful words. They indicate the tremendous hostility Saul had toward the church of his day. His feelings were violent, and he was bent on destroying the Lord's disciples and their faith.

Saul's hostility toward believers was such that he was not content to eliminate the movement in Jerusalem alone. He wanted to keep it from spreading. With a letter from the high priest, Saul went to the region of Damascus for the sole purpose of seeking those who belonged to the "Way" (verse 2). It was his intent to root out these Christians and bring them back to Jerusalem as prisoners. In reality, he was fighting a losing battle. How could he possibly stop the movement of the Spirit of God?

Satan is never ready to recognize defeat. Though he knows he can never defeat the purposes of a sovereign God, he is not distracted from his effort. Though he fights a losing battle, he fights it to the end.

Saul's heart was filled with hatred and bitterness. His intent was to wipe out the cause of Christ. It was here that the Lord met him. You do not have to be good to meet the Lord. The Lord meets us right where we are. He meets us in our sin and rebellion. This is what happened to Saul. In the midst of Saul's rebellion, when he was not even looking for Jesus, Jesus was seeking Saul.

The Lord revealed himself to Saul in a bright light and a voice from heaven. The impact of the light was such that it forced Saul to the ground. He heard a voice from heaven speaking to him. This voice asked Saul: "Why do you persecute me?" (verse 4). Saul did not know who was speaking to him, but he addressed the voice as Lord. Saul knew that this being who spoke to him was worthy of his respect and adoration. The voice identified itself: "I am Jesus, whom you are persecuting" (verse 5).

Saul persecuted the Lord Jesus by persecuting the church. Matthew 25:40 tells us: "The King will reply, 'I tell you the truth, whatever you did for one of the least of these brothers of mine, you did for me.'" There is a connection between the Lord Jesus and his people. What we do to God's people, we do to God. What a difference it would make in our dealings with other Christians if we understood this principle. When I insult a brother in the Lord, I am in insulting the Lord. Saul had to realize that he was fighting against the Lord himself.

The Lord is concerned about what happens to me. He knows the pain I feel. Those who insult and persecute me will have to answer to the Lord for what they have done. I am unworthy of this great care and concern. The reality of the matter, however, is that he cares deeply for me and when someone touches me, they touch the "apple of his eye" (Zechariah 2:8).

The Lord told Saul to go into the city where he would be shown what to do. When he stood on his feet again, he could no longer see. This persecutor of the church had been doing his utmost to destroy the work that the Holy Spirit had begun. Saul had been Satan's instrument. But now the enemy of the church was helpless and blind. Saul was forced to bow the knee to the one he sought to persecute.

What a sovereign and almighty God we serve! No matter how cruel and harsh the enemy, our God is able to overcome. He is greater than any enemy who can come against us.

Saul's traveling companions took him by the hand and led him into the city. So broken was he by this encounter that for three days Saul sat in total blindness, eating nothing. During those three days, the Lord spoke with Saul. From verse 12 we understand that he had a vision during this time about a man who would come to him and heal him of his blindness. We can imagine that these days were very intense for Saul. No doubt, he did much thinking about what had happened to him and about his rebellion against the Lord Jesus. Saul probably shed a few tears for his sins against the church of Christ.

There was a man in the city of Damascus named Ananias. The Lord spoke to him and told him to go to the house where Saul was staying and place his hands on him so that Saul could be healed and filled with the Holy Spirit. Ananias had heard about this man Saul. He had heard that Saul had come to arrest those who believed in the name of the Lord Jesus. Ananias had also heard about what Saul had done to the saints at Jerusalem. Ananias was not quite sure about going to see Saul, so he questioned the Lord on this matter.

The Lord revealed to Ananias that this man who had persecuted the church was to be an instrument to bring the gospel to the Gentile world. Saul would suffer much for the cause of the gospel. We can only imagine the shock of this statement to Ananias. God can use anyone to accomplish his purposes. How often we have our own ideas of what God will or will not do. Who would have thought that God would break Saul and make him a believer?

In obedience to the Lord, Ananias laid his hands on Saul. Immediately, something like scales fell from Saul's eyes and his sight was restored. When he got up, he was baptized as a sign of his newfound relationship and commitment to the Lord he at one time sought to persecute.

It was not long before Saul began to preach in the synagogues about his new faith. He boldly told all who listened that Jesus was the Christ, the Son of God. Verse 22 tells us that Saul grew more and more powerful. Notice here that while he was filled with the Holy Spirit, he still grew in power. Even those who are filled with the Holy Spirit need to grow in their abilities to be instruments of God's power. Saul's testimony baffled the people in Damascus who knew that he had come to persecute the church.

It is interesting to compare Saul's experience of being empowered by the Holy Spirit with the experience of Peter. Both Peter and Saul knew the empowering of the Holy Spirit. Peter's first message resulted in over two thousand souls being added to the church. Saul's first sermon, on the other hand, did not have the same impact. What does this tell us about the ministry of the Holy Spirit? Does it not tell us that the Holy Spirit cannot be put in a box? He works as he sees fit in the lives of each individual.

While Saul's early messages did not initially win thousands to the Lord, they did, nonetheless, have an impact on the city of Damascus. The Jews decided that this man should die. They decided that they would seek to kill him before he persuaded too many people to become followers of Christ. The hunter had become the hunted. Day and night they watched the city gates, hoping to catch him as he left. Knowing of their plans, the believers in Damascus lowered Saul over the city wall in a basket, enabling him to escape and return to Jerusalem.

In Jerusalem Saul tried to join with the believers, but they were afraid of him. There in Jerusalem he was known for his persecution of the church. The Christians there found it hard to believe that he had come to faith in Christ. Quite possibly they felt he was resorting to trickery to infiltrate their community. These were not easy times for Saul. He was neither accepted by the Jews nor the Christians. He had nowhere to go.

It was Barnabas who came to the aid of Saul in his moment of trial. Barnabas was willing to take the risk that the conversion of Saul was genuine. He took Saul to the apostles and told them how he had come to know the Lord and how he had been a fearless witness in the region of Damascus. The result was that the church in Jerusalem finally accepted Saul.

For a time Saul moved about freely in the city. He even began to debate with the Grecian Jews about the Lord Jesus. This led to the Grecian Jews seeking to take Saul's life. The believers came to his rescue and sent him off to the region of Tarsus. We will not hear any more about Saul until chapter 13 of the book of Acts. We are not told what Saul did in Tarsus, but he was not immediately thrust into the ministry. Like Moses, Saul was given time to develop his spiritual life.

It is not easy to go through a period of silence as Saul did. Having discovered this incredible new power, Saul was thrust into the wilderness where he was forced to wait on God. Here he would be humbled and better equipped before being entrusted with his ministry. Like Moses, Saul needed first to learn some lessons in the wilderness.

The passage goes on to tell us that with the absence of

Saul, the church enjoyed a time of relative peace. It would appear from this verse that the key figure in the persecution had been Saul himself. He had been Satan's instrument to destroy the work that God was doing. Satan's efforts were again thwarted when the God removed Satan's key man and brought him to a saving knowledge of the Lord Jesus Christ. Again, the Lord won the battle.

For Consideration:

- Why do you suppose there are certain people we never think to pray for or witness to? What challenge does this meditation have for us in this regard?

- Take a moment to consider how you treat your fellow believers. What connection is there between your relationship with them and your relationship with God, according to this meditation?

- What struggles are you facing now? What does this section of Scripture tell you about God's ability to deal with that problem?

For Prayer:

- Thank the Lord that he is greater than your worst enemy.

- Have you been praying for someone for a long time? Thank the Lord for what he did in Saul's life. Ask him to do the same thing in the life of your friend.

18

Aeneas and Tabitha

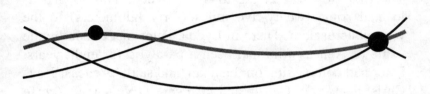

Read Acts 9:32–43

F ollowing the brief description of Saul's conversion and his first days as a believer, the book of Acts returns to spotlighting the activities of the apostle Peter. From Acts 8:1 we are led to believe that the apostles stayed in Jerusalem during the time of the persecution. In Acts 8:14 we learn that Peter went to Samaria to see what God was doing through Philip. After his time in Samaria, Peter returned to Jerusalem (8:25). We understand from Acts 9:32 that Peter traveled around the country, visiting the saints who had been scattered because of the persecution.

We are not told the purpose of these visits. We may assume, however, that Peter's visits had a twofold objective. These visits would have been a source of encouragement to the scattered believers separated from each other because of the persecution. During these visits, the apostle Peter would have had opportunity to bring encouragement and hope. Maybe some of these believers had relatives in prison because of their faith. Clearly, these people needed to be encouraged in their faith. Secondly, these visits would have served to maintain the purity of the church. The scattered believers not only needed to be encouraged but they also needed to be taught the truth of the gospel. These apostolic visits would have given Peter the opportunity to instruct the scattered disciples in the ways of truth. This ministry was vital to the doctrinal purity of the church.

We have a record in this passage of two of Peter's stops. The first stop was in the town of Lydda. This town was located some twenty-five miles (forty kilometers) to the west of Jerusalem. There in Lydda, Peter met a man by the name of Aeneas who had been a paralytic for eight years. Peter had compassion on this man, and said: "Aeneas, Jesus Christ heals you. Get up and take care of your mat" (verse 34). Immediately, the man stood up and was healed.

It is important for us to note what Peter said to Aeneas. He told him that Jesus Christ healed him. Peter did not want any confusion in this matter. Peter did not want the glory for himself. He saw himself as a mere instrument through which the power of the Lord Jesus could flow.

There is an important lesson in this for us. How often have we felt the prick of pride when the Lord used us to accomplish something for his kingdom? There are times when we begin to feel that the Lord's work really depends on us.

There are two principles that we need to learn from this example of Peter. The first principle is that we need to expect the Lord to work through us. Peter was not surprised when God actually healed Aeneas. We ought to live our lives expecting God to work in us to touch others. While we cannot force God to do what we want him to do, we can be the instruments through whom he does what he wants to do.

The second principle is one of humility. Peter gave all

the glory to God. He knew that it was not because of him that Aeneas was healed. All the praise was given to the Lord Jesus. It was Jesus who healed Aeneas (verse 34). Peter found the balance between expectation and humility.

Notice the result of this miracle. The people in that region saw what had happened and turned to the Lord. What would have happened if Peter had not been so clear about the fact that it was the Lord Jesus alone who had healed this man? Would the crowd have turned to the Lord Jesus or would they have turned to Peter? What a dangerous thing it is to take the glory for ourselves and thereby set ourselves up against the Lord.

From Lydda Peter traveled to Joppa. Joppa was less than twelve miles (twenty kilometers) from Lydda. The believers in the region had invited Peter to come to them. A certain lady named Tabitha had died. She had had a very impressive ministry in the region of Joppa. She was known for her good works and for helping the poor. From verse 39 we understand that she had made clothes for the widows and the poor. She was well known and much appreciated in the community. When she became sick and died, the whole town grieved.

It is interesting to note that even though Tabitha's body had been washed and prepared for the funeral, the believers still asked Peter to come quickly. There was the expectation that the Lord could use Peter to raise the dead. These believers felt that Tabitha's ministry was still needed. When Peter arrived, the town had gathered to pay their last respects. The widows were in mourning. They showed Peter the robes Tabitha had made for them. Peter sent them all out of the room. When he was alone, he got down on his knees and prayed. Then turning to Tabitha, he said: "Tabitha, get up" (verse 40).

What was the subject of Peter's prayer? We are not told. Notice, however, that when he finished praying, he simply commanded Tabitha to get up. There was confidence in his voice. This leads me to believe that Peter's prayer had something to do with seeking the will of the Lord for Tabitha's life. By prayer Peter prepared his own heart and sought God's direction. When he had the assurance of God's will, he simply stood up and commanded her to arise. How often do we rush into things without seeking the will of God? Peter first spent time seeking the will of God, and only then did he step out boldly to accomplish that will. Tabitha opened her eyes and sat up. Peter took her by the hand and brought her to the people. Many people believed in the Lord Jesus because of this great miracle.

Have you ever had times when you have given up hope? If there ever were a time to give up hope, it would have been when the doctor pronounced Tabitha dead. Nothing could be done for her then. Maybe your church is spiritually dead. Maybe you have a son or daughter who is spiritually dead and unable to trust the Lord. Maybe it is a situation that you are living in that seems very hopeless. We see here that God can reach down into the deadness of our situations and bring life and hope again. Where hopelessness reigns, God can bring hope and healing. Do not despair in asking. God is the God of the impossible.

For Consideration:

- Consider Peter's proclamation: "Jesus Christ heals you." Do you think that this is the will of the Lord in all situations? Why do you suppose Peter could say this with assurance to Aeneas and Tabitha?

- How do we know when God has answered no to our prayers? When should we keep trusting God for a specific answer?

- How often have you been guilty of rushing ahead of God and not first seeking his direction and guidance in prayer or in the decisions of every day?

For Prayer:

- Are there things for which you have given up hope? Remember how Peter prayed against all odds. Recommit these matters to the Lord today.

- Thank God that there is nothing too difficult for him.

- Take a moment to consider the ministry that God has given to you today. What is God's heart for your ministry? Are you moving as he leads you, or are you simply doing what you think is best? Take a moment to pray that God would lead you and give you clear direction in that ministry.

19

Broken Traditions

Read Acts 10:1–29

In this chapter we meet a centurion named Cornelius. A centurion was a Roman military official who was usually in charge of one hundred soldiers. He was a very important man in the society. Cornelius was attached to what was known as the Italian Regiment.

The passage tells us that Cornelius and his family were "God-fearing" individuals. It should be noted here that there is a difference between being one who fears God and a true Christian. Cornelius and his family feared or reverenced God, but they had not yet become true believers. It is important that we make this distinction. Many people go to church and do what is right. They even pray and read the Bible. This does not mean, however, that they are Christians. Cornelius and his family were devout in their religion. Cornelius prayed on a regular basis to the Lord God and gave to the poor. In verse 3 we see that the Lord even spoke to him in a vision. It is amazing to see how close we can get to the Lord without really knowing him. Jesus tells us in Matthew 7 that some may even prophesy, do signs and wonders, or even drive out demons in the name of the Lord and still not belong to him: "Many will say to me on that day, 'Lord, Lord, did we not prophesy in your name, and in your name drive out demons and perform many miracles?' Then I will tell them plainly, 'I never knew you. Away from me, you evildoers!'" (Matthew 7:22–23).

One day at three o'clock in the afternoon, Cornelius had a vision. In this vision he saw an angel. Cornelius was terrified. The angel told him that God had heard his prayers and seen his gifts to the poor. God was pleased with Cornelius and his family. The angel told him to send for Simon Peter (verse 5).

We need to notice some things in these verses. Why did God send his angel to Cornelius? Here was a man who was truly searching for God. Like the eunuch Philip met on the desert road, this man was ready to receive the Lord Jesus. The angel appeared to Cornelius because his heart had been prepared. He was looking for the truth.

Notice that the angel told Cornelius to contact the apostle Peter. Why would the angel ask him to get in touch with Peter? If Cornelius needed to hear the message of salvation through the Lord Jesus and his work, why could the angel not have told him? Why did Peter have to be disturbed? These verses say something to us about God's purposes. God has not given the preaching of the gospel to angels. He has given this ministry to you and me. Angels may help us or direct us, but if men and women are going to hear the gospel, it is up to us to tell them. It was for this reason that the angel told Cornelius to call for Peter.

When the angel left, Cornelius called for two of his servants and a soldier. He explained everything to them and sent them to Joppa to search for Peter. As the men were making their way to Joppa, God was preparing Peter for what was about to happen. Peter went up to the roof to pray while the noon meal was being prepared. As he prayed he fell into a trance in which he saw a vision of a large sheet coming down from heaven. Inside the sheet Peter could see all kinds of animals, reptiles, and birds. One look at these animals and Peter was repulsed. These were unclean animals. Peter then heard a voice saying: "Get up, Peter. Kill and eat" (verse 13). He responded: "Surely not, Lord! . . . I have never eaten anything impure or unclean" (verse 14). The voice then said: "Do not call anything impure that God has made clean" (verse 15). Peter was clearly confused. He knew what the Law of Moses stated on this issue.

Altogether, this sheet appeared to Peter three times. Each time the voice repeated the same thing. The repetition of this vision three times may simply have served to drive the point home to Peter. It is interesting to note, however, that while Peter was trying to understand this vision, the Spirit of God told him that three men were downstairs waiting for him. Is there any connection between the repetition of this vision three times and the three Gentiles waiting for him downstairs? What God was saying to Peter was that the Gentiles were now clean. Peter was to listen to these men and return with them to their master's house. God was preparing Peter for the task he had for him. God had gone ahead of these three men to prepare Peter for their arrival. This is the exciting thing about the work of sharing the gospel. While God expects us to go, he does not leave us to fend for ourselves. He goes before us to prepare hearts.

In obedience to the prompting of the Spirit of God, Peter went downstairs to meet these men. They informed him that they had come from Cornelius. They told Peter about the angel who had come to Cornelius in a vision. Peter invited the men in as his guests.

The next day Peter and some of the believers from the region of Joppa went with Cornelius's servants. When they arrived in Caesarea, they found that Cornelius had called his friends and relatives together to hear what Peter had to say. When Peter walked into the house, Cornelius fell at his feet in reverence. To Cornelius, Peter was a man sent from God. Peter reminded him that he was a mere man and neither expected nor desired any such signs of reverence. Peter told Cornelius to stand up.

Upon entering the house, Peter reminded Cornelius that it was against the Law of Moses for a Jew to step inside a Gentile home. Peter was willing to go inside only because God had spoken to him in a vision about this matter. God had shown him through this vision that he should not call any person impure or unclean.

We can only imagine, however, how hard it would have been for Peter to break with the tradition he had grown up with in order to go into a Gentile home. Have you ever found yourself in the position of Peter? Maybe you have grown up in a certain tradition, but God is showing you something else. I have met people who would rather die than change their tradition. Even though they know what God is saying to them, they refuse to listen. Peter could have refused to enter into a Gentile home. This could very likely have been the first such home he had ever entered. The Lord had a purpose for him on the other side of that door. He would never see the fulfillment of that purpose until he put aside his tradition and went through the door of this Gentile house. Could it be that you are in the same situation today? Are you standing at the doorstep of opportunity and blessing? The only thing that is holding back that blessing is the fact that you are not willing to break with a particular sin or tradition. Maybe God is speaking to you right now. Maybe you can see yourself in Peter's shoes. May God give you the victory today.

For Consideration:

- What kind of barriers or traditions can hold us back from accomplishing the will of God today?

- Is there anyone today that you need to speak to about the Lord?

- Are there people you need to be reconciled with today? Who are these individuals?

- What does this section of Scripture teach us about hearing from God in the work of evangelism?

- What encouragement do you receive from the fact that the Lord God goes ahead of you?

For Prayer:

- Ask the Lord for forgiveness for the times you have refused to step through those doors of opportunity to share your faith.

- Ask the Lord to help you deal with those individuals you consider unclean. Ask him to heal these relationships and make things right.

- Ask God to teach you how to listen to his leading in your life.

20

The Conversion of Cornelius

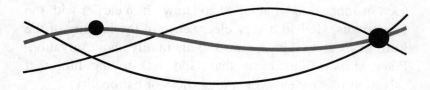

Read Acts 10:30–48

P eter stood before Cornelius and his family. God had made it clear to Peter that he had a purpose for him in this Gentile home. It was not yet clear, however, what God wanted him to do. Peter had asked Cornelius why he had called him.

Cornelius explained that a man in shining clothes had appeared and told him to send for Peter. Although Cornelius was not sure why he should call for Peter, he believed that Peter had a message from God, and so he had gathered his entire family and his close friends to hear it.

What should Peter say? What message did God want Peter to give to these Gentiles? God had been dealing with Peter about this issue. Peter seemed to know what it was that these people need. He knew deep in his heart that God was asking him to tell them about the salvation the Lord Jesus had come to offer.

Up to this point, Peter had believed that the Jews were

the only chosen people of God and that salvation was for the Jews. God had been dealing with him on this issue. Earlier, Peter and John had seen undeniable proof that the Holy Spirit had come to the Samaritans (Acts 8). God had also shown Peter in a vision at Simon's house that the Gentiles were no longer to be considered unclean (Acts 10:9–15). This was something radical. It went against everything Peter had previously understood. It went against his tradition and upbringing. As he traveled to the home of Cornelius, Peter must have been thinking very much about the vision he had seen in Joppa and what God had shown him earlier with the Samaritans. He had a very clear sense of the leading of the Lord to speak to this Gentile and his family about salvation. Peter knew in his heart that God was telling him that salvation was for everyone, regardless of nationality.

Peter's message appears to have been brief and to the point. This section of Scripture presents the simple message of the gospel. Let's look at this message in greater detail.

Peace with God through the Lord Jesus (verse 36)

What is the message of the gospel? It is a message of peace with God through the work of the Lord Jesus. We are all guilty before God. As guilty sinners, we are under his judgment. What a terrifying thing this is. We deserve God's wrath, but Jesus came to reconcile us to God. He came to give us peace with God.

Jesus Came to Offer Freedom from the Power of the Devil (verse 38)

We were all bound by the evil one who kept us in spiritual darkness. We could not deliver ourselves from his hands. He had sunk his teeth into the back of our necks and was dragging us off to hell. We were bound by sin and its evil effects on our bodies and souls. We could do nothing about it. Jesus alone had the power to release us from Satan and his power. He came to set us free.

Jesus Died on the Cross of Calvary (verse 39)

How did Jesus release us from the power of the evil one? He took our place on the cross of Calvary. We were condemned by God. We should have died, but Jesus stood in our place. He took your sin and mine on his shoulders and paid the penalty for us. Now Satan has no claim or authority over us. Those who trust in Christ's death are set free from the penalty and bondage of sin.

Jesus Rose from the Dead (verse 40)

Jesus did not remain in the grave. Not only did he pay the penalty for our sins, he also conquered the grave. His resurrection was proof that God accepted his offering. Jesus is alive today. Because he lives, we have hope in him.

Jesus Is the Judge of the Living and the Dead (verse 42)

As the living Savior, he is now our judge. We are accountable to him for what we do with his offer of peace with God. All must stand before him to give an account of personal decisions. To reject his offer of salvation is to perish without hope.

All Who Turn to Jesus Can Have Forgiveness of Sin (verse 43)

While rejecting what Jesus offers results in eternal death, reaching out to him and accepting what he freely gives results in forgiveness of sins. We can do nothing to merit this forgiveness. It is a gift offered to all who will accept it. All we have to do is receive what Jesus offers us.

This, briefly, was the message that the apostle Peter shared with the Gentiles who had gathered that day. Even as Peter spoke, the Holy Spirit came on these Gentiles. The Jewish believers who had come with Peter from Joppa were astonished when they saw these Gentiles speaking in tongues and praising God. This was a very clear sign that Gentile believers had been given the same Spirit as the Jewish believers.

Seeing that God had accepted the Gentiles and placed his Spirit within them, Peter knew that no one had any right to reject them as brothers and sisters in Christ. He suggested that they be baptized with water as a sign of their identification with the Lord Jesus and full heirs of salvation, along with the Jews.

While the Jews may not have been too eager to accept these Gentile converts, it was evident that the Lord had accepted them. To the Jewish mind, Gentiles were unworthy of the message of salvation. The Lord, however, is much more willing to accept people than we are. Many clashes could be avoided if we only realized this fact. Can we reject someone the Lord has accepted?

For Consideration:

- Could you present a simple message of salvation to someone who asked you? Reconsider Peter's presentation of the gospel. What are the basic elements of his gospel presentation?

- What comfort do you take in the fact that the Lord accepts all races and nationalities?

- Are there people you have difficulty loving or accepting? Does the Lord love these individuals? What should your response be to them?

For Prayer:

• Ask the Lord to give you an opportunity to present the message of salvation to someone this week.

• Ask the Lord to open your heart to any prejudices you might have. Ask him to help you to love and accept those whom he loves, regardless of race, practice, or social standing.

• Ask God to give you the grace to be willing to step out and accept his ways, as Peter did.

21

The Church of Antioch

Read Acts 11:1–30

By the time Peter arrived in Jerusalem, the news of the conversion of the Gentiles had preceded him. Not everyone received this news with joy. The Jewish believers still struggled with their old prejudices. They could not understand how the Gentiles could receive the same salvation as the Jews. After all, were the Jews not the chosen people of God? The Gentiles had never observed the laws of Moses. How could they ever be considered equal to the Jews?

Those who did not receive this news well criticized Peter for breaking the law. They had heard that he had entered the home of a Gentile and eaten with him. Peter was asked to defend his actions before the Jewish Christians of Jerusalem.

Peter explained to his accusers what had happened in Caesarea. He told them that when he was in Joppa, he had seen a vision of a great sheet descending from heaven and containing all sorts of unclean animals. He stated that he had heard the voice of God saying: "Do not call anything impure that God has made clean" (verse 9). He told them that three men had appeared at the home of Simon the tanner with a story about an angel appearing to their master and telling him to call for Peter. He explained that the Lord told him to go with these men, which he did, taking six brothers with him. When Peter had arrived at the Gentile home, Cornelius had told him about the angel's command to send for Peter. Peter further explained to his accusers that the Holy Spirit had come on these Gentiles when they heard the message of salvation, even as the Spirit had come on the Jews at Pentecost. The believers who had come with Peter from Joppa witnessed what God had done in the lives of these Gentiles. We cannot hear of these details without having a sense that the Lord God was in all these events.

After explaining these things to his accusers, Peter told them that he had accepted these Gentiles as fellow believers. How could Peter refuse to accept those the Lord had accepted and given the same gift of the Holy Spirit as he had given the Jews? The sign that Gentiles belonged to God was the fact that they were baptized with the Spirit of God.

What are Christians? Christians are people who have received new life by means of the Spirit of God coming to live within them. This indwelling is only possible because these individuals have been forgiven and cleansed by the blood of Christ. Peter and the believers from Joppa saw first-hand the evidence of the presence of the Holy Spirit in the lives of these Gentiles and therefore had come to believe without a doubt that to oppose Gentile salvation was to oppose God himself (verse 17).

What could the Jewish Christians of Jerusalem say to all of this? They had to recognize that God had placed his Spirit in the lives of the uncircumcised. To refuse to fellowship with them would be to reject the work of God. Their objections were calmed by Peter's explanation, and their hearts were filled with praise and gratitude to God because he had reached out even to the Gentiles with the gifts of repentance and salvation.

Evidence of this mentality of salvation for the Jews alone was not only to be found in the city of Jerusalem but also among those who had been scattered during the persecution in the time of Stephen. These scattered believers had traveled as far as Phoenicia, Cyprus, and Antioch in Syria. Phoenicia was located to the immediate northeast of Palestine. Antioch was about three hundred miles (five hundred kilometers) to the north of Jerusalem. Cyprus was an island some two hundred and fifty miles (four hundred kilometers) to the northwest of Jerusalem in the Mediterranean Sea. The believers who had been dispersed because of the persecution preached the good news in these areas. What is important for us to note, however, is that they preached the gospel to the Jews only (verse 19).

It was some men from Cyprus and Cyrene (North Africa) who went to Antioch and preached the good news to the Greeks. The result of this early missionary activity was that many believed. This was the start of what was to be a very influential church. From this church in Antioch, the gospel would spread to the Gentile world. It was from Antioch that the greatest missionaries of that day were called to missionary service. Is it not ironic that the names of the ones who started this church are not even mentioned in this passage? These men, however, were key figures in the missionary movement of the early church. They dared to leave their own lands to preach the gospel to Greek-speaking Gentiles. These were men who risked the disapproval of their Jewish Christian brothers and sisters to see that the Gentiles heard about the salvation offered them in Jesus Christ. They believed that God had a place in his heart for the Greeks as well as the Jews. While their names did not go down in history, their impact is still being felt today.

So great was the work of God in the city of Antioch that the apostles heard about it in Jerusalem (verse 22). They sent Barnabas to see what was going on. When Barnabas arrived in Antioch, he saw very clear evidence of the moving of the Spirit of God. He encouraged the believers in their walk with the Lord. Many came to the Lord Jesus through the ministry of Barnabas in Antioch.

Very quickly Barnabas felt the need for help. He remembered that Saul was in Tarsus, some one hundred and twenty miles (two hundred kilometers) away. Barnabas traveled to Tarsus to bring Saul to Antioch, and for a year Barnabas and Paul worked together there. During this time the new converts were taught the Word of God. The church grew in number and maturity under their ministry. It was there in Antioch that believers received the name "Christians" (followers of Christ) for the first time (verse 26).

During those days some prophets came to Antioch from Jerusalem. One of these prophets was a man named Agabus, who prophesied that there would be a great famine over the entire Roman world. This famine took place under the reign of Claudius. Notice the response of the believers in Antioch. They felt compelled to do something about this need. Each of them gave as they were able so that their brothers and sisters would be cared for in their need. When the offering was gathered, these believers in Antioch sent their own pastors with it to the elders in Judea. Notice that the Gentiles had no problem accepting and serving their Jewish brothers and sisters in Christ.

We see here that the Spirit of God was working in the life of this church in Antioch. Like the early Jewish believers in Jerusalem, these Gentile believers had a heart for those in need. They were willing to sacrifice their own comfort to provide for fellow Christians. The passage indicates that this was not a decision forced on them. They gave "each according to his ability . . . for the brothers living in Judea" (verse 29). The disciples in Antioch appear to have been of one mind in this endeavor. Saul and Barnabas had ministered to them, and now it was time for them to minister to others. I have no doubt that these Syrian Christians took great joy in reaching out to fellow believers in need. This is a sign of a maturing church.

The believers in Antioch, under the ministry of Barnabas and Saul, were beginning to understand that God had brought them together not only to encourage one another in the faith but also to minister to those in need. Here was a church that recognized its mission. These disciples realized that all God had given them was to be used for his glory. While they too may have suffered the consequences of the famine, they were concerned for their brothers and sisters in other places. It is this outward vision that would keep them alive. A church that does not look beyond its four walls is a church that will surely die.

There is something else worthy of mentioning about this church in Antioch. From what we can gather, it was a church composed of both Jews and Gentiles working together in harmony. Barriers had been broken and all the disciples accepted each other as brothers and sisters in Christ. God's Spirit was moving in this church. Was this in part because they were all able to put aside their prejudices?

We are living in an age where true believers are separated by countless denominational and doctrinal barriers. Sometimes we don't even notice the problems of our brothers and sisters outside our church doors. The church of Antioch has much to teach us about concern for those outside our four walls. It has much to teach us about love and acceptance of each other's differences. This was a church that became important in sending out missionaries. May God give to us churches like the church in Antioch.

For Consideration:

- How do you recognize a true work of the Lord?

- To what extent does your church have a vision for those beyond its four walls? What can be done to improve this?

- What barriers separate true believers today?

For Prayer:

- Ask the Lord to break any barriers that cause division in the body of Christ.

- Ask the Lord to help you set your eyes more on the needs around you and less on yourself.

- Ask the Lord to open doors for your church to reach out in new and fresh ways.

22

Further Persecution

Read Acts 12:1–25

During the days of Herod, the church went through another wave of persecution. These disciples had already been scattered by a persecution that had broken out in Jerusalem after the stoning of Stephen. Chapter 12 records that the political leaders joined in an effort to hinder the work of the church. Behind all this, of course, was Satan who was not content to watch God's people advance his holy cause.

This new wave of persecution began when Herod arrested some Christians. Verse 1 tells us that it was his intent to persecute them. Part of the persecution involved the killing of James, the brother of John. James was one of the twelve disciples. He had been close to Jesus and a very influential figure in the life of the early church. He was the first of the apostles to be martyred for his faith. We can only imagine how this must have affected the church.

The Jews were ecstatic about the death of James. Herod,

wanting to please the Jews, then seized Peter and put him in prison under a heavy guard of four squads of four soldiers each (verse 4). One can only wonder why it was necessary for Herod to have Peter guarded by sixteen soldiers. Was he preparing for some attempt on the part of the church to break him out by force? Had he heard about how the apostles had escaped from prison when the angel of God opened the gates and set them free (Acts 5:19)? There is no doubt that the life of Peter was at stake. Peter was to be brought to trial after the Jewish Passover.

The church did not attempt to break Peter out of prison by force but instead went to God about this problem. Verse 5 tells us that the church prayed earnestly to God for Peter. Time passed. The date of the trial approached. Soon it was the night before Peter's trial. Was God going to do anything? The faith of the church was being stretched. What should these believers do? Was this a case where it would be better to take matters into their own hands? Did God really hear the prayers of his people?

Verse 6 tells us that the very night before the trial, Peter was sleeping between two soldiers. He was bound to them with two chains. Sentries stood guard at the entrance. There was no possible chance of Peter escaping. Things looked hopeless.

In this hopeless situation an angel of God appeared. The angel told Peter to get up, put on his sandals and cloak, and follow him. I do not know about you, but I would have had some serious doubts about what the angel was saying. How was it possible for Peter to follow the angel with two guards attached to his arms, the prison doors securely locked, and armed guards watching his every move? Peter himself had trouble believing what was actually happening. Verse 9 tells us that Peter thought he was having a vision.

Obeying the voice of the angel, Peter rose to his feet. The chains that bound him to the guards fell from his wrists.

Peter and the angel passed the first and the second guards, and then the iron gate leading to the city opened by itself, allowing them to go through it. The angel took him the length of one street from the prison and left him alone. It was not until this point that Peter realized that what had happened was not a vision. He had really escaped. We are not told how long he stood there on the street.

God had frustrated the plans of Herod and the Jews. This must have been a very special moment for Peter. He was, no doubt, amazed at the grace of God in delivering him from the hand of the enemy. Herod and his sixteen soldiers were not enough to hold Peter against the will of God. By prayer, the believers had accomplished far more than they could have accomplished by physical force.

What a powerful lesson there is for us in this story. How often do we take matters into our own hands? How many of us would have been devising ingenious plans for how we could break Peter out of prison? Others would have simply given up and claimed that it must be the will of God that Peter die. Waiting on God is not always easy. Far more is accomplished, however, in prayer and waiting on the Lord than is accomplished in human wisdom and strength.

Having come to himself, Peter decided to go to Mary's house where they had gathered for prayer (verse 12). When he arrived, he knocked on the door. The servant girl came to answer the door. When she recognized his voice, she ran back into the house to tell the others that Peter was at the door. In her excitement she had not opened the door to let him in.

There are some important details that we do not want to miss in this account. First, verse 6 tells us that it was the night before the trial of Peter. While we do not know the exact time of night, Peter was asleep. Sometime ago I had the privilege of spending a month in Haiti. Very often, there was no electricity in the city where I was staying. As a result, meetings were held when there was still light. Verse 12, however, tells us that though it was night, the believers had gathered for prayer. When Peter arrived at the home of Mary at this peculiar hour, the believers were in the midst of a prayer meeting. How long had this meeting been going on? We are not told. What is clear is that they refused to stop petitioning the throne room of heaven for the life of Peter. While they were praying, the Lord sent his angel.

The second thing we do not want to miss is the fact that the servant girl did not immediately open the door to Peter. You will remember that this was a time of persecution. It would not have been wise to open the door for just anyone. Saul had dragged believers from their homes to prison. The believers were forced to live in hiding.

It is interesting to hear the response of the believers to the announcement of Rhoda, the servant girl. "You're out of your mind," they told her (verse 15). Even when she kept insisting, they refused to believe. They told her that it must be Peter's angel. We can only admire the faith of this servant girl. When the other disciples refused to believe that God had answered their prayers, she alone stood firm.

There is a certain humor here in verse 16. While the believers were arguing about who was at the door, Peter kept knocking. Eventually someone had the idea that it might be good to open the door to see if it really was Peter. When they opened the door and discovered that it was Peter, they were astonished.

Peter did not stay with them very long, but he did tell them how the Lord had answered their prayers. We can only imagine how the faith of these Christians was strengthened by this testimony of Peter. Did they spend the rest of the night in thanksgiving and praise? We are not told. One thing is certain—with all the excitement, they would not have had much sleep that night.

It is interesting to note that the only other reference to

Peter in the book of Acts is found in Acts 15, where he was present at the council of Jerusalem. The Biblical account of Peter's life ends abruptly with this description of his miraculous rescue. He disappears behind the scenes.

In the morning at the Roman prison, the situation was quite tense. The morning brought real confusion. Herod made a thorough search for Peter, but could not find him. He ordered the execution of all the guards. The law stated that they were to pay with their lives for the escape of a prisoner.

As for Herod, the final verses of chapter 12 tell us how his life ended. Herod left Judea for the city of Caesarea. It appears that he had trouble with the inhabitants of Tyre and Sidon. These cities were important Phoenician trading ports. Tyre and Sidon depended on the support of Herod for their commerce and food supply. Having enlisted the support of Blastus, who was a trusted personal servant of Herod, some of the inhabitants of these two cities decided to meet with Herod in Caesarea to resolve their differences.

On this appointed day Herod appeared in his royal robes before the gathered people. He sat on a throne and delivered a public address. As the crowd listened to him, they cried out: "This is the voice of a god, not a man" (verse 21).

We have already seen that Herod had tried to please the crowd by arresting the apostle Peter. Herod seems to have been a man who thrived on the approval of his subjects. He took great delight in their praise and adoration. On this occasion his heart was lifted up in pride. He rejoiced to hear the praise of these people. He failed to recognize that all he possessed had come from God. Herod took all the praise for himself and in so doing blasphemed the name of God. Even as he soaked up this praise and adoration, an angel of the Lord struck him down. God made it clear to the people of Tyre, Sidon, and Caesarea that Herod was far from being a god. There before his subjects, he collapsed in acute pain. He was humbled before all who honored him as a god.

Verse 23 tells us that he was eaten by worms and died. We can have confidence in Luke's diagnosis as a doctor. Some commentators see here an infestation of roundworms or tape worms. Some roundworms can grow to a length of sixteen inches (forty centimeters). They feed on the fluids of the intestines. If they obstruct the intestines, they can cause severe pain, the vomiting of worms, and even death. Herod's end was not pleasant.

With the death of Herod, the Word of God continued to spread. Nothing could stop the movement of the Spirit of God. Satan had attacked the church, but again his key instrument was removed. If God is for us, who can be against us?

For Consideration:

• How do we know when we need to wait on the Lord and when we need to step out boldly in faith?

• Have you ever been surprised when God actually answered your prayer? Why are we surprised to see these answers?

• What do we learn from the death of Herod about what God thinks of pride?

• What do we learn here about the commitment of the early church to prayer?

For Prayer:

• Have you been praying to God for a particular request that has not yet been answered? Take courage from this passage and bring that request again to the Lord.

- Has the Lord delivered you from a "prison" in your life? Take time to thank him for this miracle.

- Thank God that he is greater than the most powerful enemy that Satan can bring against you.

- Ask the Lord to increase your faith in light of what you have learned in this chapter.

23
Paul's First Missionary Journey
Part 1: Call and Ministry in Cyprus

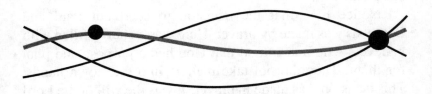

Read Acts 13:1–12

In the last meditation we saw how Peter was miraculously rescued from the hand of Herod, who sought to kill him. In this chapter the focus shifts from Peter to Paul. (In verse 9 of this chapter, Saul becomes known as Paul. To avoid confusion we will refer to him as Paul throughout this passage.) For the remainder of the book of Acts, we will trace the events of the life of Paul and his missionary journeys.

The ministry of Paul began in the city of Antioch (9:26). Paul and Barnabas had been serving in this city for at least a year. The church grew tremendously under their ministry. It grew in number, maturity, and influence in the Christian world. Over time the Lord gave the church many gifted teachers and prophets. In verse 1 we have the names of five such men who were involved in ministry in the church of Antioch.

Maybe it was the fact that there were so many gifted

teachers and prophets in this one location that caused the leadership to wonder what their next step should be as a church. Was it right for one church to have so many teachers and prophets when there were whole villages that had never even heard the message of the gospel? Were these questions on their minds as they fasted and prayed to the Lord (verse 2)? What is clear from the passage is that as they came with open minds seeking the will of the Lord, the Lord told them to set apart Barnabas and Paul for another work he had in store for them.

Notice here that the decision to send out Paul and Barnabas was made by prayer. Here was a church filled with believers who understood that God had a purpose and plan for them. They did not take matters into their own hands. This decision was made in prayer. It was the will of the Lord for the church in Antioch to send out Paul and Barnabas to the harvest field of human souls. This church had grown tremendously, and it was time to share that growth with others. A church can have so many committee meetings and so little prayer. A church can have lots of discussion but little listening to God. Antioch, however, was a church that was hearing from God. We need to catch this vision in our day as well.

Have you ever had a potted plant? Maybe you have had one that was in the same pot for years and appeared to thrive. As time went on, however, you began to notice that its growth came to a halt. The problem was that the pot had become too small. The roots had no place to go. The plant had reached its maximum potential in this pot. If something was not done, it would be stunted. In order to further develop, the plant had to be transplanted into a bigger pot or, better yet, divided and placed in several pots. This is what was taking place in the church of Antioch. The teachers and prophets had become too numerous. They were tripping over each other in their efforts to advance the ministry. The time had come to consider dividing up the plant and starting new works.

I have been in churches where there was an over-abundance of spiritual leaders. There are some churches where you have to place your name on a waiting list and wait your turn to use your gift, and, at the same time, there are places where the Word of the Lord is not being preached or taught at all. The church in Antioch came to realize that something needed to be done about this kind of imbalance.

Notice in this passage that the Lord chose to send out Paul and Barnabas. The Lord took two of their principle leaders. The church did not question the will of God in this matter. How often we keep the best for ourselves. When it comes to missions, we have a tendency to give what is left over. But here God took the cream of the crop. The church in Antioch owed much to the leadership of Paul and Barnabas. To lose them would be a great loss indeed. How important to you is the task of reaching the world? If you were in Antioch and had grown under the ministry of these two great men of God, how would you have felt if God decided to take them away? Does this not show us how important missions and outreach is to God?

The will of God concerning Paul and Barnabas was not questioned. Immediately, the leaders placed their hands on them and set them apart for this ministry (verse 3). After a time of prayer and fasting, Barnabas and Paul were sent off. I am sure the church was eager to see what God would do with them. There was no doubt an air of expectancy as they watched them go. The church would stand behind them in prayer as they ministered. Through these two men, many would come to know the Lord Jesus as Savior.

Paul and Barnabas left Antioch and traveled south to the port city of Seleucia. There they took a boat and sailed to the island of Cyprus. They arrived at the port city of Salamis. There were several Jewish synagogues in this city. We discover that John Mark (possibly a relative of Barnabas, according to Colossians 4:10) was with them at this time. The three men went immediately to the synagogues and preached the Word of God to the Jews. We are not told what the response of these Jews was to their message.

From the city of Salamis they crossed the entire island of Cyprus, preaching the Word of God. In verse 6 we are told that they traveled to Paphos, which was located on the other side of the island of Cyprus approximately ninety miles (one hundred and fifty kilometers) from Salamis. There they met a Jewish sorcerer and false prophet named Bar-Jesus. The word *bar* in front of a name means "the son of." Since the Greek word for Jesus and for Joshua is the same, this man was the son of a man named Jesus or Joshua. Bar-Jesus was an attendant or deputy of the Roman proconsul, Sergius Paulus. The proconsul was a Roman government official in charge of administrative and military matters.

Sergius Paulus wanted to hear what Paul and Barnabas had to say, but Satan would not let this man come to know the Lord without a fight. In Bar-Jesus, Satan had the man he needed to oppose the preaching of the gospel to Sergius Paulus. Bar-Jesus, who was also called Elymas (meaning "sorcerer"), did his best to keep Sergius Paulus from receiving the message of the gospel. Elymas, according to Paul, was a child of the devil (verse 10). In this particular case, Elymas was being used by Satan to oppose the preaching of the good news. Paul openly rebuked him as an enemy of everything that is right.

This passage presents a clash between the kingdom of God and the kingdom of Satan. Paul turned to Elymas and accused him of perverting the ways of the Lord. Paul told him that he would be struck with blindness because of his opposition to the preaching of the good news of Jesus. Immediately, Bar-Jesus was enveloped in darkness. He was left trying to find someone to lead him by the hand. All efforts on the part of Satan through Bar-Jesus to hinder the Word of God were thwarted. Bar-Jesus was in reality used of God to convince Sergius Paulus of the truth of the message Barnabas and Paul preached. Seeing what had happened to this sorcerer, Sergius Paulus believed in the Lord Jesus. He had seen a visible demonstration of Christ's power at work, and this brought him to faith.

In Cyprus there was evidence of satanic opposition to the preaching of the gospel, but the Lord proved to be more powerful than the opposition. God even used a sorcerer to advance his kingdom. The God who called Paul and Barnabas did not leave them to minister on their own. He went with them. Though Satan himself opposed them in Cyprus, they were victorious in the name of the Lord.

For Consideration:

- How does this passage demonstrate God's heart for outreach and missions?

- What kind of sacrifice would you willingly make so that the cause of the gospel could be advanced among those who have yet to hear?

- What does this passage teach us about the importance of hearing from God?

- What encouragement do you receive from the fact that God was with Paul and Barnabas in their travels? Will God abandon those he has called?

For Prayer:

- Thank the Lord that Satan is defeated in Jesus' name and that no force that is raised against us can prevail.

- Take time to pray for a location where the gospel is not being preached today.

- Thank the Lord for the spiritual leaders he has given you.

- Take a moment to pray for those whom God has sent out from your church to serve him in different capacities.

- Thank the Lord that when he calls us, he also equips us and goes with us in that calling.

24

Paul's First Missionary Journey

Part 2: Pisidian Antioch

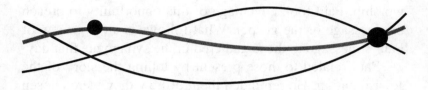

Read Acts 13:13–52

P aul, Barnabas, and John Mark had just crossed the island of Cyprus, preaching the gospel. In spite of some satanic opposition, the work of the Lord had advanced. Sergius Paulus, a Roman official, had believed in the Lord. This alone had made their time on Cyprus worthwhile. From the port city of Paphos, the missionaries sailed to Perga in the Roman province of Pamphylia. Perga was approximately one hundred and eighty miles (two hundred and eighty kilometers) to the north of Paphos.

On their arrival in Perga, John Mark left them to return to Jerusalem. We are not told why John left. From Acts 15 we understand that Paul had a hard time accepting this departure. When Paul and Barnabas decided to go on their second missionary journey, Paul refused to take John Mark along because of his desertion here in Perga. We will consider this in detail at a later point. Apart from this one incident, we have no other record of what took place in Perga.

From Perga Paul and Barnabas continued north to the city of Antioch in the region of Pisidia. This is not to be confused with the Antioch in Syria, the starting point of this missionary journey. As was their custom on the Sabbath day, Paul and Barnabas went to the synagogue. While we often consider the religion of the Old Testament to be quite formal, notice the freedom and spontaneity described in this passage. After the reading of the Law and the Prophets, the rulers of the synagogue asked Paul and Barnabas if they would like to share anything with those who had gathered for worship. Paul took advantage of this opportunity to preach the message of the gospel. What follows is an overview of Paul's message to those gathered in the synagogue that day.

Paul related to those present by telling the story of the Jewish nation. He reminded them of how they were chosen by God to be his people. God prospered them in their time of exile in Egypt and set them free with demonstrations of great power under the ministry of Moses. For forty years God endured their constant complaining as they wandered through the wilderness. Under the ministry of Joshua, God defeated seven different nations in the region of Canaan and gave this land to his people. According to Paul, these events happened over a period of four hundred and fifty years.

When God's people were safely settled in Canaan, judges governed them until the time of Samuel. During the days of Samuel, God's people asked for a king. God gave them a king by the name of Saul. He reigned for forty years. After that time God removed him as king and gave his reign to David, a man after God's own heart (verse 22). David, unlike Saul, served the Lord with his whole heart.

Following this brief history of the nation of Israel, Paul spoke about David's family. Paul told his audience that from the family of this great king, God brought to Israel the promised Savior, Jesus. John the Baptist had preceded this Savior, preaching a message of repentance. Many people were touched by John's message. John was not the promised one but announced his coming. John told people that after him would come one whose sandals he was not even worthy to untie. This one was the Savior, the Lord Jesus Christ.

Jerusalem rejected Jesus as the Savior. Though Jesus was innocent, the people of Jerusalem and their rulers had Pilate crucify him. They placed Jesus in a tomb and sealed it; however, Jesus did not stay in the tomb. God raised him from the dead. Numerous individuals saw him over the course of many days. These people then served as witnesses to the Jews that Jesus was alive.

Paul then quoted three Old Testament passages in support of what he had just said. He first reminded his listeners of the second Psalm: "You are my Son; today I have become your Father" (Psalm 2:7). Admittedly, it is difficult to see the connection between this verse and what Paul told his listeners that day. It may be best to understand what Paul is saying here in light of what he tells us in Romans 1:2–4, "The gospel he promised beforehand through his prophets in the Holy Scriptures regarding his Son, who as to his human nature was a descendant of David and who through the Spirit of holiness was declared with power to be the Son of God by his resurrection from the dead: Jesus Christ our Lord."

Paul reminded the Romans that while Jesus was the Son of God from the beginning, God declared that relationship with power when he raised Jesus from the dead. In other words, Jesus proved to the world that he was the Son of God by conquering death. Death could not hold him because he had also conquered sin. The resurrection was God's stamp of approval on the work of the Lord Jesus. God proudly declared Jesus to be his obedient and faithful Son, the very image of his own nature. Though Jesus was a human descendant of David, he was far more than this. God himself said of Jesus: "You are my Son; today I have become your Father." Paul seems to be communicating the

Father's approval of the work of Christ and the victory he accomplished on this earth.

Second, Paul went on to use a passage from Isaiah to further support his teaching on the resurrection. Isaiah 55:3 states: "Give ear and come to me; hear me, that your soul may live. I will make an everlasting covenant with you, my faithful love promised to David." This verse speaks about an everlasting covenant that God would make with his people. This was a covenant of faithful love promised to David. How was the faithful love demonstrated to God's people? In the context of the passage quoted, Isaiah spoke about forgiveness of sin, joy, peace, and prosperity (55:7, 12–13). These things God promised to David and his descendants. The question we need to ask ourselves here is, how did these promises come to us? They came by means of the work of the Lord Jesus as a descendant of David. All the covenant promises given to David, as seen in Isaiah 55:7–13 (forgiveness, joy, peace, prosperity), are fulfilled in the Lord Jesus through his work on the cross and resurrection.

The third Old Testament passage that Paul quoted was from the book of Psalms and tells us that the Holy One would not be abandoned in the grave nor would he see decay: "Because you will not abandon me to the grave, nor will you let your Holy One see decay" (Psalm 16:10). The very concept of the Messiah (the Holy One) going to the grave was beyond understanding for the average Jew. The Psalmist tells us that the Holy One would not be abandoned in the grave. This implies that he would have to go to the grave. Only those who die go to the grave. Paul was showing his listeners that the only way to understand this passage was to see it in light of the death of the Lord Jesus who died and was raised from the dead. This proved that there was a resurrection. It also proved that the Lord Jesus was the Holy One, for no one else had died and risen from the dead without undergoing corruption.

In verse 41 Paul's prayer for his listeners was that the prophecy of Habakkuk 1:5 did not come true in their lives. In this verse Habakkuk was speaking to those who scoffed at the Word of God. He told them that the Lord would do something in their midst that they would never believe, even if they were told. From the context of this prophecy in Habakkuk, we see that God was going to send the Babylonians to judge his people. The enemy would swoop down on God's people like vultures and destroy their fortified cities. Because of their unbelief, God's people would suffer discipline in a way they had never seen. Paul was saying that if his listeners rejected Jesus the Messiah, their eternal Davidic king, they too would experience this heavy hand of God's judgment.

Notice the effect of this message on the lives of the listeners. Verse 42 tells us that as Paul and Barnabas were leaving the synagogue, they were invited to return again the next Sabbath to speak further on this matter. Many of those who had heard Paul speak followed him as he left the temple, intent on finding out more about Jesus. During the week people began to speak one to another about Paul's message. Verse 44 tells us that on the Sabbath nearly the entire city gathered to hear Paul speak. The Spirit of God was obviously at work in this city.

We have seen in this book of Acts that when the Lord begins to do a work, Satan is never very far behind. Once again, Satan looked for an instrument through which to do his work. In Cyprus he had used a sorcerer. Here he chose to use the Jewish leaders. Seeing the crowds listening to Paul, these leaders were stirred with jealousy. They began to speak abusively against Paul and his message. Their intent was to make him look bad before the people so that the people would reject what he was saying.

Paul did not argue with these Jews. He told them, however, that since they refused to accept the Word, he would take it to the Gentiles. Paul reminded them that this fulfilled the prophecy of Isaiah which stated: "It is too small a thing for you to be my servant to restore the tribes of Jacob and bring back those of Israel I have kept. I will also make you a light for the Gentiles, that you may bring my salvation to the ends of the earth" (Isaiah 49:6).

When the Gentiles present heard this good news, they rejoiced. A number of them believed. Notice that it was those who had been "appointed for eternal life" who believed (verse 48). None of us would ever naturally come to the Lord of our own free will. Before we come to the Lord Jesus, the Spirit of God must work in our lives. God must touch us before we can touch him. This is what was happening here. God had spoken to certain hearts. He was calling individuals to himself. These individuals heard his voice and responded.

In spite of the opposition on the part of these Jews, the message of salvation spread throughout the region. God continued to advance his kingdom. Once again, the jealousy of the Jewish leaders was stirred up. They incited certain God-fearing women and men of high standing in the city against Paul and Barnabas. Notice that these women were called "God-fearing women" (verse 50). This does not mean that they had accepted the Lord Jesus. These women were religious, but they had not accepted the truth of the gospel. These "God-fearing" women and leading men were successful in turning the people of the city against Paul and Barnabas. This was a sign to the missionaries that it was time for them to move on to another city. They left behind in Pisidian Antioch, however, a group of joyous and Spirit-filled believers. Despite the opposition against the apostles, God had accomplished everything he had intended to accomplish through them. Once again, Satan was unsuccessful in his efforts to hinder the gospel to those who had been appointed for eternal life.

For Consideration:

- What tactics has Satan been using in your church to keep it from growing?

- What evidence is there of the victory of the Lord in your church despite the attempts of the enemy to thwart the plan of God?

For Prayer:

- Thank the Lord that his work is moving ahead despite the efforts of Satan to destroy it.

- Ask God to give you the boldness of these apostles to stand firm despite the opposition.

- Take a moment to pray for Christian workers who are right now facing opposition in the preaching of the good news of the gospel.

25

Paul's First Missionary Journey

Part 3: Iconium, Lystra, and Derbe

Read Acts 14:1–28

We saw in the last meditation how Paul and Barnabas had been driven from the city of Pisidian Antioch by a group of jealous Jews who had stirred up the city against them. Their time in the city, however, had been fruitful. During their ministry in Pisidian Antioch, they had seen the conversion of a number of Gentiles. God had given them victory in spite of the obstacles thrown on their path. Paul and Barnabas continued on their journey to other cities.

Iconium

From Pisidian Antioch, the apostles traveled southeast to the town of Iconium (a distance of approximately seventy miles or one hundred and fifteen kilometers). There Paul and Barnabas went to the synagogue. Again they were given opportunity to speak with those who had gathered for worship. The Bible tells us that they spoke so effectively that many Jews and Gentiles believed. The question may be asked why the Gentiles were in the synagogue. These were very likely Gentiles who had converted to Judaism.

Again we see the clash between the kingdom of God and the kingdom of Satan. Satan did not give up his hold on Iconium without a fight. There had been opposition to the preaching of the gospel wherever Paul and Barnabas had gone on this missionary journey. In Cyprus it was Bar-Jesus who opposed them. In Antioch it was the jealous Jews who started a persecution against them. In Iconium the opposition came from the unbelieving Jews. These Jews stirred up the Gentiles and poisoned their minds toward Paul and Barnabas. We are not sure what the unbelievers were saying about the apostles, but we can be sure that the intention was to destroy their reputations and cast doubt on what they were preaching. It should not surprise us that the enemy resorts to lies and slander against the work of God. Satan is the father of lies (John 8:44).

Initially, this opposition did not deter the missionaries. They continued to preach the gospel boldly. The Lord himself was with them as they persevered in this ministry in Iconium. The Lord showed his presence to the inhabitants of this city by performing many signs and miracles through Paul and Barnabas (verse 3). These miracles were hard to deny. The result was that the city was divided. Some believed the gospel while others rejected it. It is clear that the city felt the impact of the Word of the Lord. I have no doubt that during this time the whole city was speaking about what Paul and Barnabas were teaching. The Spirit of God was in evidence. People's lives were being changed by the message of salvation.

Seeing the gospel's impact in the city, the Jews who opposed Paul and Barnabas decided to step up their opposition by making plans to have them stoned. Paul and Barnabas heard about this plan and decided it was time to leave. While the enemy opposed the work of the gospel in Iconium, the kingdom of God still advanced. Paul and Barnabas left behind yet another group of newly converted Christians. These individuals in turn would reach out to others. From Iconium Paul and Barnabas traveled twenty miles (about thirty kilometers) south to the city of Lystra, where they continued to preach the good news of the gospel.

Lystra

It was in Lystra that Paul and Barnabas would experience the greatest opposition of their first missionary journey. It all began when they met a man lame from birth. He had heard Paul speak. Paul looked at him and saw that he had the faith to be healed. Speaking directly to the man, Paul told him to get up on his feet. The man jumped to his feet and began to walk (verse 10). It is hard to imagine the emotions that must have been running through this man's mind as he stood on his feet and walked for the very first time in his life.

The crowd was astonished at what they saw. They had never seen such a thing. They began to shout: "The gods have come down to us in human form!" (verse 11). Barnabas they called Zeus, and because Paul was the spokesperson, they called him Hermes. A brief look at these gods will give us an understanding of the religion of the people of Lystra.

Zeus was the principle god of the Greeks. His parents were Cronus and Rhea. As the chief god, he ruled the sky. His brothers ruled the underworld and the sea. As the ruler of the sky, he was the god of weather and fertility. Stories about him tell of how he fathered many children through various women (both goddesses and human women). He often resorted to trickery to hide his infidelity from his wife. He was considered by the Greeks to be a god of power who rewarded good and evil.

Hermes was one of the sons of Zeus. He was the god of

travelers and thieves. Because of his eloquence, he became the messenger of the gods. He was a very deceitful god. He was responsible for conducting souls to the underworld.

It was into this type of religious background that the message of the gospel was being preached. The healing of the lame man had caused people to believe that Zeus and Hermes had come to them in person. The priest of Zeus brought bulls and wreaths in order to offer sacrifices to Paul and Barnabas. Seeing this, the apostles tore their clothes as a sign of mourning and pleaded with the people to cease from offering their sacrifices. The apostles declared that they were mere men and challenged the people of Lystra to turn from their false religion to the Lord Jesus, the true God who showered on them his kindness by giving them rain and crops. According to the Greeks, Zeus was the god of weather and fertility who provided crops in their season. But Paul told the people that it was his God who provided all this for them. Paul seems to have been culturally aware of their religious beliefs and used this knowledge to speak about the true God. However, Paul and Barnabas had great difficulty in keeping the people from sacrificing to them (verse 18).

The response to the gospel in Lystra was very different from Iconium. The enemy in Lystra was very successful in creating confusion and distracting the people from the truth of Jesus. Soon after these events, Jews from Antioch and Iconium arrived in Lystra. Their intent was clear. They did not want Paul and Barnabas to continue preaching the gospel. When these Jews arrived in Lystra, they found the city in an uproar. They stirred up the people against Paul and Barnabas. As a result Paul was stoned and dragged outside the city and left for dead.

It is interesting to note, however, that certain disciples gathered around Paul, and he got up and went back into the city. This verse should not go unnoticed. It tells us that the time Paul and Barnabas spent in Lystra did produce fruit.

Who were these disciples? Were they individuals who had believed Paul's message? When Paul and Barnabas left Lystra, they left behind yet another group of believers. Though the apostles suffered greatly in Lystra, the Word of the Lord had gone forth and individuals in this town had come to the knowledge of Christ.

Derbe

The day after being stoned and left for dead, Paul and Barnabas traveled forty miles (seventy kilometers) southeast to the city of Derbe. There Paul continued to preach the good news of Christ. What is even more astonishing is that when he finished preaching in Derbe, he returned to Lystra, where he had been stoned, to strengthen the believers he had left behind. From Lystra he returned to Iconium and Antioch, strengthening and exhorting the new believers to persevere in their walks with the Lord. He reminded them that it would not be easy for them to follow the Lord. The scars Paul carried on his body testified to this fact.

Before returning home Paul and Barnabas appointed elders in each of the established churches. These elders understood the difficulties of the ministry. They had seen how Paul had suffered for the preaching of the gospel. They knew that they too risked suffering for the cause of Christ. Paul did not apologize for this. He simply told them to persevere. Then with prayer and fasting, Paul and Barnabas committed to the Lord's care all these new believers and their leaders.

From Pisidian Antioch Paul and Barnabas traveled south one hundred and twenty miles (two hundred kilometers) to the towns of Perga and Attalia. Perga was the port city where John Mark had left them. Attalia was located some thirty miles (fifty kilometers) to the west of Perga. From Attalia they sailed approximately three hundred and thirty miles (five hundred and thirty kilometers) back to Antioch in Syria, where their journey had begun.

Back in Antioch they reported the things the Lord had done on their missionary journey. They shared how God had opened up a great door for the Gentiles to come to the knowledge of Christ. Paul and Barnabas remained for a long time in Antioch. Over the past months, these two men had traveled over thirteen hundred miles (two thousand one hundred kilometers). They had been verbally insulted and physically beaten because they had preached Christ. On this journey, they had seen the Lord work in miraculous ways. We do not know how many churches were planted during this journey, but we do have records of groups of believers in Pisidian Antioch (13:48–52), Iconium (14:1), Lystra (14:20), and Derbe (14:21). While we do not have a record of a church in Cyprus, we do know that at least one man came to faith in Christ on that island (13:12). Was this missionary journey a success? Because of this one journey, at least four new churches were planted, with elders in place. Many individuals (both Jews and Gentiles) came to know the Lord as their Savior. I do not know of many missionaries in our day who could boast in the Lord of such an achievement in one missionary journey. Though the opposition had been great, God proved to be greater.

For Consideration:

- Consider for a moment Paul's willingness to suffer for the cause of Christ. What do you suppose was the driving force behind this man?

- Why do you suppose Paul was not discouraged to the point of giving up this difficult work?

- What would you be willing to suffer for the cause of Christ?

- What have you had to suffer for preaching the gospel?

For Prayer:

- Take a moment to pray for a particular missionary or Christian worker. Ask the Lord to keep this person faithful through trials and difficulties.

- Ask the Lord to give you more boldness in your witness for him.

- Commit yourself afresh to serve the Lord, no matter the cost.

26

The Jerusalem Council

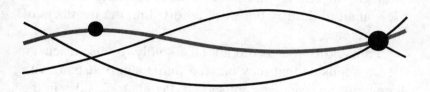

Read Acts 15:1–35

We have seen in the last three meditations how
Satan was actively involved in the process
of hindering the ministry of the gospel. Paul
and Barnabas suffered greatly under the opposition of the
enemy, but the grace of God had sustained them during
their missionary journey. The problems did not stop when
they returned home to Syrian Antioch. Satan continued in
his efforts to destroy the work of God. The clash between
the kingdom of God and the kingdom of Satan never stops.
We need to be constantly aware of his tactics. He will stop
at nothing in his futile effort to entirely destroy the work of
God.

The attack of the enemy came to Antioch in the form
of Jewish teachers who taught that unless a man was
circumcised according to the custom of Moses, he could
not be saved. The teaching caused quite a stir among the
believers in Antioch. It forced them to ask a number of

questions. Could an uncircumcised Gentile be a Christian? What was the place of the Law of Moses in the life of the believer? Were Gentile believers inferior in any way to Jewish believers? It is quite easy to see what the results of this could have been in the church. Satan was sowing seeds of doctrinal dissension and pride. How easy it would have been for this to divide the church of Antioch by setting one believer against another. This would have destroyed the impact of the church for the cause of Christ. Satan knew how strategic the church of Antioch was in reaching the world. He sought to destroy the work by dividing the members of this church.

Paul and Barnabas did not take kindly to false teachers. Verse 2 tells us that they entered into a sharp dispute with them, but the issue was not settled. People took sides in the debate, and there was no agreement. The church decided to send Paul and Barnabas to Jerusalem to meet with the apostles there and discuss this issue. Paul and Barnabas would have to travel over one hundred and eighty miles (three hundred kilometers) to Jerusalem to find a solution to this problem. This shows us the impact these false teachers had on the church of Antioch.

As they traveled to Jerusalem, Paul and Barnabas met with fellow believers in the regions of Phoenicia and Samaria. The apostles shared how the Lord had opened a door to the Gentiles. The news of the spread of the gospel brought great joy to the hearts of these believers. On arriving in Jerusalem, Paul and Barnabas informed the church there as well what God had been doing through them.

In the Jerusalem church were believers who belonged to the sect of the Pharisees. While these individuals had accepted the Lord, they believed that it was still necessary for Christians to keep all the Law of Moses. Obviously, the salvation of Gentiles through the ministries of Peter, Paul, and Barnabas had caused theological problems for the

Jewish church. There was much confusion over this matter. The apostles and elders met to discuss the issue. This was not an easy issue for them. Verse 7 leads us to understand that they discussed the issue for a long time. We get the impression that they initially did not come to an agreement. These Jews had grown up with the Law. It was through the Law that God had revealed himself to Israel. There were stiff penalties for all who refused to obey this Law. Could they simply throw it away now that they were believers in Jesus Christ?

It was partially the testimonies of Peter, Paul, and Barnabas that gave the church council the needed answer. Peter stood up in the assembly and told of salvation among the Gentiles he had witnessed. He recounted the story of the Gentile family of Cornelius and how the Spirit of God came on them in his presence. In Peter's mind this could only mean one thing. It meant that the Lord had accepted the Gentiles as they were, even though they did not practice the Law of Moses. God's Spirit had been given to both those who practiced the Law and those who did not. The conclusion he drew from this was that a person did not have to live under the Law to receive the Holy Spirit. God made no distinction between the Jew, who was under the Law, and Gentile, who was free from the Law. Peter's conclusion, therefore, was that if God did not put restrictions and requirements on the Gentiles before he gave them his Spirit, then neither should the church place restrictions on them. Salvation was by grace and not by observation of the Law.

Peter is telling us here that God accepts us as we are. Salvation is by grace. It is a gift given to the undeserving. Salvation has nothing to do with how we live our life. It has nothing to do with how we dress or how we look. It has nothing to do with our color or race. It has nothing to do with how often we go to church. It has nothing to do with what we have done for the Lord or how we have treated our neighbor. In fact, salvation has nothing to do with us at all. When it comes to salvation, God does not take our character or achievements into account. We can live as a pious Jew or a pagan Gentile and it will not affect whether God will save us or not. God will pour out his Spirit on anyone he desires. There is nothing we can do to make ourselves more acceptable to God. We are totally dependent on his grace and mercy.

This was a radical statement for Peter to make to a group of Jewish believers. He was telling them in effect that the Law of Moses could not save them. Notice in verse 12 that the whole assembly became silent. Paul and Barnabas then told the council of their experiences and how God had brought faith to the Gentiles through signs and wonders.

I can see in this silence the movement of the Spirit of God. Naturally, this was a very divisive topic, which could have divided the assembly. Humanly speaking, the meeting could have erupted in angry, physical arguments. (Maybe you have been to a few church meetings like this.) Tempers could have flared as people got upset. Some could have walked out in a spirit of bitterness while others could have called on the traditions of the fathers, saying that what was good enough for Abraham was good enough for them. Still others could have threatened to leave the church if tradition changed. But none of this took place. Instead, there was a spirit of unity that is the envy of every general church meeting. The only way we can account for this is that the Spirit of God was moving in their midst as they made this all-important decision.

Next, James stood up with a word from the Lord (verse 13). He quoted Amos 9:11–12 in which God spoke through the prophet Amos to tell his people that he would one day rebuild David's fallen tent (symbol of God's people). In that day both Jews and Gentiles would seek the Lord. James confirmed from Scripture what Peter and Paul had been experiencing in their missionary endeavors. James then made the motion that they not place the Gentiles under the yoke of the Law. In recommending this he was saying that it was no longer necessary for the Gentiles to live under the Law of Moses to be saved and glorify God in their lives.

This recommendation was not without its problems. What about those Jewish believers who continued to practice the Law of Moses? How could they fellowship in the same church with Gentiles who felt no need to keep this Law? Would this not create confusion? Would it not place an obstacle before those who still felt an obligation to practice the Law of God? To remedy this James suggested that certain measures be taken. He recommended first that the Gentile believers abstain from eating meat sacrificed to idols or meat that had been strangled and the eating of blood.

Paul would later write in his first letter to the Corinthians that while there is nothing wrong with eating these things in themselves, this could be a stumbling block for another person. Paul instructed: "Eat anything sold in the meat market without raising questions of conscience, for, 'The earth is the Lord's, and everything in it.' If some unbeliever invites you to a meal and you want to go, eat whatever is put before you without raising questions of conscience. But if anyone says to you, 'This has been offered in sacrifice,' then do not eat it, both for the sake of the man who told you and for conscience' sake— the other man's conscience, I mean, not yours. For why should my freedom be judged by another's conscience?" (1 Corinthians 10:25–29).

Gentiles were to be encouraged to refrain from eating certain things so that they would not be a stumbling block to Jewish believers. Gentiles were to do this out of respect for their brothers and sisters, not because they were required to do so to glorify God.

The second recommendation of James was that the Gentiles abstain from sexual immorality. We need to remember that the Gentiles who came to the Lord in the days of Paul and Barnabas came from very immoral backgrounds. The Greek gods they worshiped were themselves guilty of immorality. We have already mentioned that Zeus, their principle god, had children through many different women (both human and goddess). Zeus resorted to deceit and trickery in order to hide his unfaithfulness from his wife. The standard by which these Gentiles had formerly lived differed vastly from the standard laid out in the Word of God. James mentioned this because of his knowledge of the cultural background of the Gentiles. He challenged them to be obedient to the Word of the Lord with regard to their moral standards.

Verse 21 supports the idea that the reason these particular issues were mentioned by James was because of the Jewish believers in their midst and not because the council wanted to place Gentiles under the Law. Moses was still being read in the synagogues each Sabbath. The Gentiles were to be sensitive to the Jews in these Mosaic matters and not openly seek trouble. Gentiles were to refrain from eating certain foods, not because of Law but out of a sense of respect for their fellow believers.

The recommendations of James were approved. Verse 22 tells us that the whole church decided to send men to Antioch with Paul and Barnabas to announce the decision of the council. Notice that the verse tells us that the "whole" church decided to do this. There was harmony in this matter. This was nothing short of the ministry of the Spirit of God.

Judas and Silas were chosen to go with Paul and Barnabas to Antioch and deliver a letter written by the apostles and elders explaining the decision of the council. Verse 28 is of particular interest to us. The letter stated that it seemed good to the Holy Spirit that the apostles and elders not place a burden on the Gentiles. The council acknowledged a conscious awareness of the ministry of the Holy Spirit during the meeting. The final resolution was the result of this ministry. That this was God's decision had been confirmed to the council in three ways.

First, the decision was based on the experiences of Peter, Paul, and Barnabas. Doors were opening and God's Spirit was being poured out. Great things were happening among the Gentiles. Miracles, signs, and wonders were in evidence. These things could not be explained in any other way but by a movement of the Spirit of God. These experiences told the elders and apostles that God was in the process of doing something wonderful.

Second, the council did not base its decision on the testimonies and experiences of Peter, Paul, and Barnabas alone. James took the council to the Word of God. James showed from the Scriptures that what was taking place was prophesied by the prophet Amos. The Word of God supported the experiences being reported. If the Scriptures had contradicted the experiences of Peter, Paul, and Barnabas, the council's conclusion would never have been made. The Scriptures themselves testified to the validity of the experiences among the Gentiles.

Third, there was the confirmation of the Holy Spirit's presence in their midst. Throughout this meeting, there was a real sense of his ministry and leading. The harmony experienced that day was a sign of his presence. The experience of God's presence was such that the leaders could say at the end of the meeting that it seemed good to the Holy Spirit to place no burden on the Gentiles. This decision was not of human origin. They all knew that this was what the Spirit of God wanted.

The church of Antioch rejoiced when the letter from the council was read (verse 31). The presence of the Spirit was evident in the church in Antioch as it dealt with this final decision. There is no record of dissension or bitterness. There is no record of anyone saying, "I told you so." All we hear is that the church rejoiced to know that Gentiles were all accepted before the Lord apart from the Law. Silas and Judas stayed a certain time with the church in Antioch to encourage these believers in the faith, and then they returned to Jerusalem. Paul and Barnabas remained in Antioch, teaching and preaching the Word.

Once again, we see that the attack of the enemy being thwarted. This attack could have set believer against believer. It could have caused a whole church to fall into doctrinal error. Instead, the church in Antioch became an example for us all. Here in Antioch both Jews and Gentiles served together. They did not always see things eye to eye, and they had their disagreements because they came from different backgrounds. For Satan this was the ideal situation for causing dissension and discord. The Spirit of God, however, brought harmony and respect for one another. Do you want to know if the Spirit of God is moving in your church? Ask yourself if the believers love and respect one another in their differences.

For Consideration:

- Are you facing a difficult decision in your life now? What does this passage teach you about how to know the will of God?

- Is it possible for us to be still living under the Law today? Explain.

- What is the difference between living under law and living under grace?

- What do we learn here about how Satan tries to divide us as believers?

For Prayer:

- Praise the Lord that he accepts you just as you are.

- Pray that the spirit of unity and harmony experienced in the church of Jerusalem in this passage would be the experience of your local church.

- Ask the Lord to help you to put aside your personal preferences and prejudices. Ask him to make you willing to accept his clear revealed will and purpose.

27

Paul's Second Missionary Journey

Part 1: The Journey Begins

Read Acts 15:36–41

Paul and Barnabas had been in Antioch for some time. Paul decided that it was time for them to return to the towns they had visited on their first missionary journey to see how they were doing. As we read the letters of Paul in the New Testament, we can see that he appears to have been constantly concerned about how his converts were doing. When he could not visit them personally, he took the time to write. No other apostle wrote as many letters to his converts as did the apostle Paul. In his letters to the various churches, he told them that they were constantly on his mind. He wanted to see them grow in their faith. He was deeply concerned that these new converts might fall away from the Lord or be led astray by false teachers. His heart overflowed with fatherly concern for the spiritual condition of the believers in the churches he established.

Barnabas, as you may recall, was an encourager. When everyone else in the city of Jerusalem had refused to accept the newly converted Saul (Paul), Barnabas had come to his aid (9:27). Barnabas had introduced Paul to the apostles and explained to them how he had been converted to Christ. Barnabas had gone to Tarsus to get Paul to help him in the work in Antioch (11:25). Barnabas had faithfully stood by Paul's side as they faced the persecutions of their first missionary journey (13:14). He had stood with Paul as they defended their actions before the council in Jerusalem. Barnabas had been there with Paul from the beginning. Together they formed what appears to have been a perfect missionary team.

Barnabas agreed with Paul that they needed to return and visit the churches they had established. Barnabas recommended that they take John Mark with them on this journey. As you may recall, John Mark had started out with Paul and Barnabas on their first missionary journey but deserted them (13:13). The question of whether John Mark should join them on this second journey caused real conflict between the two missionaries. While Barnabas wanted to give John Mark another chance, Paul did not want to take him because he had not proven faithful on their last journey. Paul and Barnabas simply could not agree on this issue. The debate was so sharp that they decided to split company and go their own ways. Barnabas would take John Mark, and Paul would take Silas.

There has been much debate over who was right in this situation. This, however, is not a black and white issue. Probably one of the greatest lessons we need to learn in the Christian life is that there is very often more than one answer to a given question. As believers, we will not always agree on issues. This does not mean, however, that one person is right and the other wrong. While we cannot pretend to understand everything that was going through the minds of Paul and Barnabas, let's attempt to look at this case through the eyes of each of these two missionaries.

As we have mentioned, Barnabas was an encourager. His heart may have been heavy when he thought about what John Mark was going through. John Mark had deserted the team on the first missionary journey, but that did not disqualify him from missionary service. In Christ there was forgiveness. John Mark was perhaps better prepared for this second journey. Maybe the last time he simply had not known what to expect. It seems that Barnabas was confident that with a little encouragement, John Mark could make a very valuable companion. John Mark needed a second chance to see a missionary journey through to the end. If he did not get a second chance, he might go through life feeling defeated. Going on this journey might give John Mark the closure he needed. It would build his confidence in what God could do through him. Barnabas may have felt that it was necessary for John Mark's growth in Christ.

Paul, on the other hand, saw things in a different light. He was well aware of the difficulties of the journey before him. On his first missionary journey, he had been stoned and left for dead outside the city of Lystra. Everywhere he and Barnabas had gone, persecution had sprung up against them. Paul's intention was to return to the churches he had started. The people in those cities knew him. Paul and his companions risked their lives by returning to these cities. This was not a place for John Mark who had deserted them even before things had gotten difficult. Paul was not saying that John Mark could never again be useful in the service of the Lord. Paul may simply have felt that this was not the journey for him. John Mark could, no doubt, be useful somewhere else. Possibly even at a later point, he could join Paul but not so soon after he had deserted him. John Mark needed time to mature. A second failure might prove too much for him and discourage him even further.

Where would you have stood on this question? This

division between Paul and Barnabas was not a black and white issue. Both men had something valid to say.

I wonder what it would have been like for these missionaries to minister after having parted company. What would be going through the mind of John Mark? What were his feelings toward Paul and his harsh attitude toward him? Would this have placed a barrier between them as brothers? What was Barnabas feeling? After all he had gone through for Paul, why could Paul not do the same for John Mark? How was Paul feeling in this situation? Did he wrestle with accepting the decision of Barnabas? What relationship existed between Paul and Barnabas at this point? These questions remain unanswered. It certainly was an uncomfortable beginning for their second missionary journey.

Satan must have been overjoyed to see such division. It is important, however, to understand that the Lord God is sovereign in these situations. In spite of what appears to be taking place on the outside, God is still working out his purposes. He even uses the sins of people to accomplish his purposes in the end. Notice what takes place here. Instead of one team of three people going on a missionary journey, we now have two teams. In this way the missionaries would cover more territory and reach more people.

A second thing to notice is that God knew what sort of tension would have existed between John Mark and Paul. While John Mark needed to be encouraged and matured in his faith, Paul was not the man to do the job. John Mark needed time alone with Barnabas. While we are not told what took place on the missionary journey of Barnabas and John Mark, it is interesting to note that later Paul would have a change of opinion about John Mark. In Colossians 4:10 Paul asked the Colossians to welcome this brother. In 2 Timothy 4:11 Paul, in his solitude, called for John Mark because he found him to be very helpful in ministry. Obviously, Barnabas did have a very positive impact on the life of John Mark who flourished and became very useful to the newly established churches.

Maybe you have found yourself in a very similar situation. Maybe you have fallen on your face. There is hope for you here. John Mark got back on his feet, persevered, and became a very important figure in the life of the early church. Maybe you need to follow his example. Maybe you know someone who has fallen. Could it be that God is calling you to be a Barnabas to that person?

Finally, we see here that God used this confrontation to bring another person into the missionary force. Silas left with Paul on this second missionary journey. Like John Mark, Silas would not be the same after this time spent ministering. He would return home a greater man of God and would become a useful instrument in the hands of God. While the team of Paul and Barnabas had been highly effective, it was time for them to split up and pass on the vision to others. God used this confrontation to double the missionary force and to extend the missionary vision of the church.

God used this disagreement between Paul and Barnabas to accomplish his purposes. He continues to do this in our day. I do not know what you have been through in your life. I do know, however, that God is sovereign over all your pain and trials. He allows them to take place and he uses them to accomplish something good. Often, time alone will tell the good things that God has accomplished through pain. Trust him in these difficulties. He knows what he is doing.

For Consideration:

- What differences of opinion exist today among sincere believers? Is God using these differences to bring glory to his name? Explain.

- What does this meditation teach you about differences that exist between you and a brother or sister in Christ?

- Have you ever had a problem or trial that God used to accomplish great good in your life? Explain.

For Prayer:

- Praise God today that he will use your present pain to accomplish great things for his glory.

- Ask the Lord to help you respect the legitimate decisions of brothers and sisters in Christ, even though they may differ from your way of thinking.

- Take a moment to pray for brothers or sisters in another church. Ask God to expand their vision and witness.

28

Paul's Second Missionary Journey

Part 2: Timothy and the Call to Macedonia

Read Acts 16:1–10

Having separated from Barnabas, Paul left with Silas for his second missionary journey. From chapter 15 we understand that Barnabas and John Mark sailed for the island of Cyprus, following the same route they had followed on the first missionary journey. Paul and Silas traveled by land, in the opposite direction. They traveled northward through the region of Syria and Cilicia and arrived in the cities of Derbe and Lystra, where Paul had planted churches on the first journey. We know nothing of what happened in these cities. We can assume, however, that Paul would have spent time with the believers, strengthening and encouraging them to continue in the Lord.

It was in Lystra that Paul met a young man by the name of Timothy whose mother was a Jewish believer and whose father was Greek. We are not told whether his father was a believer. In later writings Paul spoke very highly of Timothy's mother and grandmother: "I have been reminded of your sincere faith, which first lived in your grandmother Lois and in your mother Eunice and, I am persuaded, now lives in you also" (2 Timothy 1:5).

Timothy's grandmother and mother would have encouraged him in his faith. Paul was so impressed with the young man that he wanted to take him on his missionary journey. We do not know how old Timothy was when he went with Paul. When Paul later wrote to him, he told Timothy that he was not to let anyone look down on his youth: "Don't let anyone look down on you because you are young, but set an example for the believers in speech, in life, in love, in faith and in purity" (1 Timothy 4:12).

This would indicate that when they first met, Timothy was quite young. Despite Timothy's youth, Paul saw something appealing in him. This was the beginning of a lifelong companionship. Paul would eventually consider Timothy to be his own son in the faith. He had great confidence in Timothy as a man of God. He would leave Timothy in the city of Ephesus to be a pastor to a newly established yet troubled church.

In chapter 15 Paul had refused to take John Mark on his missionary journey. We should not get the idea from this that Paul was not interested in mentoring young converts. This passage would indicate that the opposite was true. Probably what we should understand from this is that discipleship is a very complex issue. We all have different personalities. There are some people whom I can disciple and minister to because of my personality and way of thinking, while some other people would not respond to my methods. They need someone else. John Mark needed Barnabas. Timothy needed Paul. Even the Lord Jesus had three disciples to whom he ministered in a deeper way than the others. The body of Christ is such that we need each other. One person cannot do all the work. We each have different areas of ministry. There are individuals whom you can touch simply because of the way God made you.

Verse 3 tells us that Paul insisted that Timothy be circumcised. This seems to run contrary to the decision made by the council in Jerusalem, which had determined that it was not necessary for a Gentile believer to be circumcised. Why then did Paul think circumcision was necessary for Timothy? This was done to aid Timothy's acceptance by the Jews and to allow him access to the synagogues where Paul and Silas would be preaching. If Timothy was going to be effective in his ministry with Paul, he needed to be able to go into the synagogues with him and preach. Paul's decision here seems to have been practically motivated. The Gentiles would have had no particular problem with the fact that Timothy was circumcised, but the Jews would not have found it easy to accept the message of an uncircumcised Gentile. Therefore, in order not to put a stumbling block before those who would listen to his message, Timothy was circumcised.

It is interesting to note that as Paul, Silas, and Timothy traveled from one town to another, they spoke about the decision of the council in Jerusalem, which was that salvation was for the Gentiles as well as for the Jews. There was salvation apart from the Law of Moses. An individual did not need to be circumcised to be saved. Paul preached a message of freedom from the Law, and yet Paul had insisted on the circumcision of Timothy. Does this appear to be hypocritical? What we need to understand here is that Timothy's circumcision was not motivated by Law so much as it was by compassion for those to whom he would minister. While Paul understood personal freedom from the Law, he refused to allow that freedom to hinder the presentation of the gospel. Paul was willing to practice the Law out of compassion for those still under the Law in order to reach them with the message of the gospel. His motto was this: "To the weak I became weak, to win the weak. I have become all things to all men so that by all possible means I might save some" (1 Corinthians 9:22).

While the apostle Paul was uncompromising in his personal convictions, he refused to let secondary matters stand in the way of reaching the world with the message of the gospel. We too have our personal comfort zones. We like things to be done in certain ways. God is far bigger than our personal liberties. He is not limited to our traditions and belief structures. He works in ways we could never imagine. Paul was willing to be stretched. He was willing to let the Lord do things in ways he was not personally comfortable with. He never compromised his doctrine. He was unwavering in his stand for the truth. Paul was willing, however, to step outside his comfort zones.

How often is the advance of the gospel hindered just because we do not feel comfortable with the method? Jesus himself appeared unorthodox in his approach. He made religious people cringe. He stretched their boundaries. If Jesus or the apostle Paul were here today, I am convinced that many churches would cast them aside because of their methods. May we learn the lesson that Paul teaches us here in this passage. Notice the result of Paul's method. Churches were strengthened and grew in faith and number. They grew because Christ was being promoted above traditions and personal preferences.

As Paul and his two companions ministered, they traveled throughout the region of Phrygia and Galatia. The Lord had a very definite route for them to follow. Verse 6 tells us that Holy Spirit hindered them from going to the region of Asia. In verse 7 the Spirit also hindered them from going into the region of Bithynia. Being kept from going to Asia to the south and Bithynia to the north and having already come from the east, the three had only one direction to go—west. They traveled as far west as they could go without getting on a boat and came to the coastal town of Troas. There the

Spirit of God revealed to Paul the direction he needed to take. In a vision that night, Paul saw a man from the region of Macedonia calling out to him to come over and help them. On seeing this vision, Paul knew right away that the Lord was calling the missionary team to Macedonia.

Verses 6–10 give us an idea of the leading of the Holy Spirit in this missionary journey. Notice that there were times when they attempted to go to a certain area but were hindered by the Spirit of God. They took initiatives but were sensitive to the fact that God might have other plans. This does not mean that they were wrong in taking the initiative. Everything they did was bathed in prayer. They committed their daily decisions to the Lord, expecting him to open or close doors according to his will. When they decided to move in a certain direction and the Spirit of the Lord hindered them, they stopped in their tracks and turned around. We see here a cooperation of human reason and will with the greater will of God.

What we learn from this passage is how important it is for us to allow God to be Lord in our lives. Sometimes this means putting aside our personal preferences. Sometimes it means bending in secondary issues to allow God to work in ways we never imagined. Other times it means allowing him to change our plans. At all times, however, it means submitting to his way of doing things and expecting him to be involved in our lives as we minister or plan for ministry.

For Consideration:

- In what areas must we be uncompromising? What would you consider secondary issues?

- Have we hindered the work of God's Spirit by our unbending allegiance to secondary issues? Explain.

- What does this passage teach us about the Lord's leading in our lives?

For Prayer:

- Ask the Lord to give you a "Timothy" to minister to today.

- Ask God to enable you to be more in tune with his Spirit, even when this means a real stretch for you in your comfort zones.

- Thank the Lord that he has not left us to minister on our own but goes before us to direct and enable us.

- Ask the Lord to help you to have his priorities. Ask him to forgive you for the times when you have allowed your personal issues to stand in the way of advancing the gospel.

29

Paul's Second Missionary Journey

Part 3: Philippi

Read Acts 16:11–40

H aving received a very clear word from the Lord, the missionaries boarded a ship and sailed to the island of Samothrace, about sixty miles (ninety-five kilometers) from Troas. The next day they sailed to Neapolis, a distance of approximately seventy miles (one hundred and fifteen kilometers). From Neapolis they traveled to Philippi, a neighboring city. From verse 12 we understand that Philippi was a Roman colony and the principal city in the district of Macedonia. God had a wonderful plan for this very busy and influential city.

On the Sabbath Paul and his companions went outside the city to a river where they expected to find a place of prayer. It is obvious from this incident that the Jewish community in Philippi was not large enough to have established a synagogue. The small band of Jews in the area had found a quiet place by a river where they could go to offer prayers on their holy day. Paul heard about this place and set out to look for it. When he arrived he found a group of women gathered for prayer. One of these women was named Lydia. She was not from the city of Philippi but from Thyatira, a city famous for its purple cloth. Lydia had very likely come to Philippi to carry on her trade. We understand from verse 14 that she was a worshiper of God. We need to understand, however, that though she worshiped the true God, she was not a Christian.

As she listened to the apostle Paul, the Lord opened her heart and she received the Word. Notice that it is the Lord who opens hearts. The act of saving a soul is a miracle. It requires the direct intervention of God in the life of a lost sinner. It requires giving sight to the spiritually blind and new life to the spiritually dead. There is no greater miracle than the salvation of a soul. God is calling each of us to this work. The exciting thing about this work is that it does not depend on us. All we do is make ourselves available to God, and he does the rest. Paul shared the message; God opened the heart.

Verse 15 tells us that both Lydia and her household were baptized. Did she return home and share the message of the gospel with the other members of her family? This would certainly have been very natural. In verse 40 we see that before leaving the region of Philippi, Paul and Silas met with the "brothers" in the house of Lydia. The term "brothers" is used in the book of Acts to refer to those who accepted the Lord Jesus. This would seem to indicate that Lydia's testimony and Paul's preaching did have some effect on this household and the community. Lydia's household committed to following the Lord Jesus and identified with him in baptism. Lydia's home became the base of operations for Paul's work in Philippi.

Paul continued to go to the place of prayer outside the city. On one occasion he met a slave girl possessed by an evil spirit that enabled her to predict the future. Her owners were able to use this power for their own profit. The girl followed the apostle and his co-workers, shouting as she went: "These men are servants of the Most High God, who are telling you the way to be saved" (verse 17). Our first impression of this might be to praise the Lord. Here was a young girl calling people to listen to the preaching of the apostle. It may surprise us, therefore, to see Paul turn around and rebuke the evil spirit within her. It appears that what she was speaking was not from the Lord but from the devil. There is an important warning for us here. Listen to what Jesus tells us in Matthew 7: "Many will say to me on that day, 'Lord, Lord, did we not prophesy in your name, and in your name drive out demons and perform many miracles?' Then I will tell them plainly, 'I never knew you. Away from me, you evildoers!'" (Matthew 7:22–23).

We understand, then, that it is possible to prophesy, cast out demons, and perform miracles and yet not belong to the Lord Jesus. In saying this we do not want to discount those true prophets who come in the name of the Lord. We do, however, need to test the spirits to see if they are really from God. What the slave girl was saying was true, but it did not come from the Lord. Don't be deceived. Satan will use every means available to place individuals within the church who do not know the Lord. Once they are inside, they can do the damage he wants them to do.

Paul knew that things are not always as they appear. In the name of Jesus Christ, the demon left the young slave girl. Her owners did not appreciate what Paul had done. Seeing that their hope of profit was gone, they seized Paul and Silas and dragged them to the marketplace to face the authorities. They accused Paul and Silas of throwing the city into an uproar and advocating customs that were unlawful for Roman citizens. The crowd joined in the accusations, and the authorities decided to have Paul and Silas beaten.

After a severe whipping, they were thrown in prison and put in stocks.

Notice how Paul and Silas passed their time in jail: they prayed and sang hymns. This went on until midnight. As they were worshiping the Lord, there was a great earthquake and the prison was shaken. The doors were flung open and all chains were loosened. There is a powerful example for us here. Paul and Silas could have given up in defeat. After all, they were in prison, and their future looked dismal. They could have blamed God and doubted his goodness because of what had just taken place in their lives. Instead, they rejoiced and recognize his perfect plan and purpose for them. They worshiped him through their hymns, confessing his goodness and worthiness even in these harsh trials.

Do you feel the oppression of the enemy? Are you discouraged? Has life dealt you a bad hand? Maybe you need to learn the lesson Paul and Silas learned that night. Could it be that in your pain you doubt the goodness of God? Could it be that you are living in defeat because you have refused to accept your trial as being a gift from a sovereign God for your good? Maybe today you need to learn to praise the Lord in your trial. God always has your best interest at heart. Thank him for that today. All too often, we become prisoners of our own attitudes. I recently had the opportunity to speak at a meeting in a town some distance away. The worship leader was completely blind. As I watched him lead worship, I was amazed at his happy and joyful attitude. I have known people to become bitter and angry because of something much less than physical blindness. My blind friend had learned to praise the Lord in his trial. Though physically restricted, he was spiritually free from bitterness, anger, and resentment. I believe he was free because he had learned to trust the Lord and worship him in whatever situation he had found himself. Worship and anger cannot walk hand in hand. We can choose to be angry or we can choose to worship and trust the Lord. What we decide will determine whether we live bound in wrong attitudes or free in Christ.

The jailer, seeing that the prison doors were open, decided to kill himself. By Roman custom, if a prisoner escaped during a jailer's watch, that jailer would be sentenced to death. A jailer guarded his prisoners with his life. Before this man could kill himself, Paul called out to him. The jailer rushed into the prison cell and saw that all the prisoners were still there. Trembling, he fell down before Paul and asked him what he needed to do to be saved.

Why did this unconverted jailer ask this question? It may have something to do with the slave girl who had called out day after day: "These men are servants of the Most High God, who are telling you the way to be saved" (verse 17). No doubt, the jailer had heard about what this girl had said. Had this jailer wondered in his own heart if what she had said was true? She did have the ability to see things others could not see. The jailer was obviously open to the message of the gospel. What had he been thinking as Paul and Silas were singing praise to God? Had this impressed him?

Seeing that the prisoners had not escaped was the last straw for this Philippian jailer. It was as if God were speaking directly to him. This man had been ready to take his own life, but God had prompted Paul to call out to him at the right time. This keeper of the prison came rushing toward the disciples, a broken man. God met him at that moment. The jailer fell down trembling before his own prisoners, as one who had been touched by their example. One thing is certain: he saw these missionaries as messengers from God who had come to bring the message of salvation. What the slave girl had said was true.

Paul told the Philippian jailer to believe in the Lord Jesus Christ if he wanted to be saved. Remember that preaching this message was the reason why Paul was in prison. The jailer knew that believing on the Lord would not be easy in Philippi. What he had seen in these apostles, however, convinced him that it was worth believing in the Lord Jesus. God's Spirit had been working in him.

Paul had told the jailer that salvation was in Jesus alone, and that salvation was not only for him but also for his household. From verse 32, we understand that Paul took the time to explain the gospel to the other members of the jailer's household. The result of Paul's preaching, according to verse 34, was that the whole family came to believe in God. After caring for the wounds of Paul and Silas, the jailer and his household were baptized. The Philippian jailer greatly rejoiced that night, for he and his family had all come to believe in God.

In the morning the magistrates sent word to the guards to release Paul and Silas. (We do not know what happened to Timothy.) Paul refused to leave. He informed the officers that because he was a Roman citizen, their treatment of him had been illegal. He demanded an official escort to come and release them. Why was Paul not content simply to be set free? Why did he feel it necessary to seek this escort and an official apology? We can only guess what Paul's motive was. Possibly part of the answer lay in the fact that the whole city was in an uproar. We can only imagine what would have happened if Paul and Silas were placed out on the street without an escort. They would have been very likely mobbed. The escort would have guaranteed them a measure of protection to get to the house of Lydia. When the crowds would have seen the Roman escort, they would have thought twice before seeking to harm the missionary team.

The escort was given to Paul and his companions. The Romans understood, however, that they could only protect the team temporarily and so asked them to leave the city. After returning to the house of Lydia and encouraging the new converts, Paul and his companions left Philippi and continued their missionary journey. They left behind, however, a small band of believers possibly meeting in the home of Lydia. Paul would later write to this church in his epistle to the Philippians.

In this letter to the Philippians, Paul recognized that these believers had gone through difficulties (Philippians 1:27–30). There was also a problem with divisions among the believers in Philippi (Philippians 2:1–4; 4:1). They faced false teachers seeking to mislead them (Philippians 3:2–4). In spite of these difficulties, however, this church remained faithful. They were the only church to send financial aid to Paul in the early days of his missionary career (Philippians 4:14–15). Despite the difficulties and the small beginning, this church would grow to maturity and have an influence on the world for the sake of the gospel.

For Consideration:

• How can we discern who is truly a servant of God if even unbelievers can perform miracles and prophesy in the name of Jesus?

• Why do you suppose Paul and Silas sang praises in prison?

• Praise can release us from our "prisons" as well. What is it about praise and worship that sets us free?

• Notice how God used even harsh treatment and imprisonment to accomplish tremendous good in Philippi. What does this say about your problems and struggles?

• Thank the Lord for the way he directs us and goes before us in the ministry he has called us to do.

For Prayer:

- We have seen the importance of praise in this section. Take a moment just to praise the Lord for who he is and what he has done.

- Thank the Lord that he is able to work out all things for the glory of his name. Commit yourself to trusting him in your trial today.

- We see here how the Lord was so willing to use Paul and his companions. Thank the Lord that he goes before us as we minister in his name.

30

Paul's Second Missionary Journey

Part 4: Thessalonica and Berea

Read Acts 17:1–15

Thessalonica

After leaving the city of Philippi, Paul and his companions traveled westward some one hundred miles (one hundred and sixty kilometers) to the city of Thessalonica. Here in Thessalonica, unlike Philippi, there was a Jewish synagogue. As was his custom, Paul went to the synagogue to speak to those present about the message of the gospel. For three weeks Paul went to the synagogue and reasoned with the Thessalonian Jews, pointing them to the Lord Jesus and showing them from the Scriptures that the Messiah had to die and be raised again from the dead.

The result of his preaching was that certain Jews were convinced that Jesus was indeed the Messiah. Many Gentiles turned to the Lord Jesus as well as a large number of prominent women. The identity of these prominent women is uncertain. They were either very wealthy women in the community or women whose husbands were community leaders. At any rate, the preaching of the gospel was having its effect in Thessalonica. It was from these humble beginnings that the church of Thessalonica began. Paul later wrote two letters to this church. From these letters we understand that the church became a model for all the churches in the region of Macedonia (1 Thessalonians 1:7). These believers were known for their love for each other (1 Thessalonians 4:9). Like the believers in Philippi, they too had to suffer for the cause of Christ. Paul wrote them in 2 Thessalonians to encourage them in their suffering (2 Thessalonians 1:4; 2:14–15).

The establishing of churches seems to have been a high priority in the ministry of the apostle Paul, although he does not appear to have had a very complicated strategy. He shared the message of the gospel and instructed the new converts in the way of Christ. He would then leave them to carry on the work of the gospel themselves. Paul kept in touch with them by means of letters and visits. They were very often in his mind and prayers. Paul took advantage of every opportunity to get news from these churches. On other occasions he would send someone to minister to them or to help them through particular difficulties. Though he was not always with them, he cared for them at a distance.

The jealousy of the Jews in Thessalonica was stirred up when they saw so many people converting to Christianity through Paul's preaching. These Jews rounded up some bad characters in the city, encouraged them to start a riot, and then rushed to Jason's house where Paul was staying, hoping to bring him out into the angry mob. We can only guess what would have happened to Paul had they found him. Obviously, the hand of the Lord was on Paul and he was protected from this angry mob. Seeing that Paul was not there, the Jews found Jason along with some other believers and dragged them before the magistrates of the city. The Jews accused Jason of welcoming Paul and his co-workers who, according to the Jews, were troublemakers who defied Caesar's laws. These Jews went on to accuse the Christians of treason, saying that they advocated loyalty to another king by the name of Jesus. These statements threw the entire crowd into an uproar. Jason and his friends were required to pay a fine, very likely to assure the authorities that they would cause no more public disturbances of this nature. Life for these new converts was not easy, but they persevered and the Thessalonian church became a model for other churches in Macedonia.

Berea

Because of this opposition, Paul and Silas left Thessalonica by night, when they would not be seen, and went to the town of Berea located forty-five miles (seventy kilometers) southwest of Thessalonica. Upon finding the synagogue in Berea, Paul and Silas began to preach the message of the gospel of Jesus Christ. We discover that the Bereans were of more noble character than the Thessalonians because they received the message with great eagerness and examined the Scriptures to be sure that what Paul was saying was true. The result was that many Jews and Greeks in Berea believed the gospel. What was it about the Bereans that made them more open to the message of the gospel? We do not really know. Later Paul would go to Athens where the citizens were said to have enjoyed listening to new doctrines. They too were open to hearing new ideas but not so open to receiving them. In Berea, however, Paul and his companions discovered open hearts. These Bereans were interested in knowing the truth. Unlike the Athenians, whose authority was their own mind, authority for the Bereans was the Scriptures. When Paul brought them to the Scriptures, they were willing to listen. When they saw that what Paul said was directly from Scripture, they were willing to believe.

What a challenge this is for us today. How often have we

listened to our own reasoning and not to the Scriptures? How often have our traditions and personal preferences kept us from searching the Scriptures for ourselves? How often have we fallen into sin because we placed our own ideas before Scripture? We often justify our actions based on reason and not on the teaching of Scripture. The Bereans are an example for us to follow. They examined the Scriptures daily to see if what they heard was true. The Scriptures alone were their authority for life and practice.

When the Thessalonians heard that Paul was preaching the Word of God in Berea, they went there to stir up trouble against him. The Thessalonians succeeded in riling the Berean crowds against Paul in particular. Knowing that Paul's life was in danger, the believers escorted him to the coast, and from there he traveled south to the city of Athens. Silas and Timothy remained in Berea. Obviously, they were not considered as much a threat as the apostle Paul. Paul tended to rock the boat. He was aggressive in his approach. He did not care what people thought of him. We are not told what Silas and Timothy did in Berea or how long they stayed. Be assured, however, that they had opportunity to strengthen the brothers and sisters of the region in their faith. Before leaving for Athens, Paul left instructions for Silas and Timothy to join him as soon as possible. They would catch up with Paul in the city of Corinth.

So far, since his arrival in Macedonia, Paul had been forced to leave Philippi, Thessalonica, and Berea because of the opposition stirred up against him. God did not promise to make things easy for Paul; he was the object of Satan's opposition. In spite of this opposition, however, the Word of the Lord moved ahead. Three new churches were planted. While we know nothing of the group in Berea, we do have a record in the Scriptures of the growth and vitality of both the church in Philippi and Thessalonica. God moved in power through Paul. Never once have we seen Paul lose hope and become discouraged He is an example for us all. He stepped out boldly, risking his reputation and his life for the sake of the gospel. He refused to give up. His energy seems to have been without end. He was a special instrument of God. May God challenge us through his life to move out in the power of that same Spirit.

For Consideration:

- Paul remained in contact with his converts. How good are we today at following up and discipling our converts?

- Is there evidence that, unlike the Bereans, many Christians today trust human wisdom more that the authority of the Word of God? Explain.

- What stands in the way of our full acceptance of the teaching of the Word of God?

- How willing would you be to suffer what Paul suffered for the cause of Christ?

For Prayer:

- Ask the Lord for grace today to be able to let his Word be your only authority in life.

- Ask God to help you become an example for others to follow.

- Ask the Lord for strength and boldness to stand up for him.

31

Paul's Second Missionary Journey

Part 5: Athens

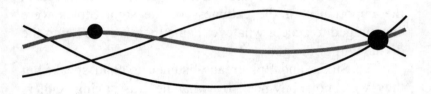

Read Acts 17:16–34

I n the last lesson we saw how the Jews from Thessalonica had conspired to force Paul to leave the city of Berea. Paul had left Berea and traveled to the city of Athens some two hundred miles (three hundred kilometers) to the south. Verse 15 tells us that Paul sent word to Timothy and Silas to join him as soon as possible.

As Paul waited in Athens for the arrival of Silas and Timothy, he became very disturbed by seeing all the idols in the city. The Greeks had a number of gods. The Athenians were a very religious people, but they did not know the truth about the Lord Jesus. As was his custom, Paul reasoned with the Jews in the synagogue, speaking to them about the Christ. He also had opportunity to speak in the marketplace each day. He used every opportunity he had to share with the Athenians the message of salvation in Jesus Christ.

It was not long before Paul attracted the attention of a group of Epicureans and Stoics. It is helpful for us examine these two philosophies. Both Epicureanism and Stoicism were founded about three hundred years before Christ's birth. The central focus of Epicureanism was the search for happiness and fulfillment in life. Epicureans encouraged the enjoyment of the good things in life and sought after tranquility of life and mind. For the Epicurean, the gods were uninterested in the everyday affairs of people on earth. In death, the soul rested undisturbed in eternal peace. The Stoics, on the other hand, felt that people needed to be freed from passion and emotion. They too believed in the importance of the calmness of the soul. Stoics were encouraged to accept whatever came their way as being the divine will of the gods.

The Stoics and Epicureans listened to Paul speak, but they were not convinced by what he was saying. Others who listened claimed that he was advocating some foreign god and wanted to hear more. Paul was brought before a meeting of the Areopagus, the highest legal council in the city of Athens. There before the greatest leaders of the city, Paul had the opportunity to share the message of the gospel. Notice in verse 21 that the Athenians were very open to listening to new ideas and philosophies. It seems that they were fascinated by new ideas.

Paul stood before the council and began his address. He recognized that the Athenians were a very religious people. He observed this by the number of idols he had seen in the city. He told them about a particular idol that had attracted his attention. It was an idol dedicated to an unknown god. Paul used this as a springboard to speak to the Athenians about the Lord Jesus. We will now examine what Paul told them about his God.

He Made the World (verse 24)

Paul's God is the creator of the world. This statement came into conflict with the religious beliefs of the

Athenians. Paul did not hesitate to proclaim the truth, even though it conflicted with the opinion and cultural ideas of his listeners.

He Is Lord of Heaven and Earth (verse 24)

Not only did Paul's God create the heavens and the earth, he is also Lord over all he created. There is no one who can take his authority. It was quite possible in the Greek religion for a god to create the world and not be in control of the world he created. This is not the case for the true God, who reigns supreme over all his creation.

He Does Not Live in Temples (verse 24)

The God whom Paul served does not live in temples. He is far bigger than that. No temple can hold him. He is everywhere present.

He Is Not Served by Human Hands (verse 25)

Many of the gods of the nations need human assistance to accomplish their purposes. This is not true of the God of Israel. He does not need humans. There is nothing that you and I could possibly give to God that he has not first given to us. We can add nothing to God's character or power. He is complete in himself. He does not depend on us.

He Gives Life to All Men (verse 25)

We are completely dependent on this God for our life and breath. We owe everything to him. Were it not for him, we would have nothing.

He Made Every Nation (verse 26)

Every nation on the face of the earth exists because of God. All power and wealth have come from him alone. This is an indication of how great and awesome he is.

He Determines the Times Set for These Nations (verse 26)

This God determines the times set for nations. That is to say, he determines how long nations will survive and when they will fall. As great and as powerful as these nations may be, God rules over them all. Even as he has fixed the day of our death, so has he determined the rise and fall of the nations around us.

He Determines the Exact Places They Should Live (verse 26)

Paul has told us that God determines the rise and fall of the nations. He also determines the exact place they should live. This may be hard for us to understand when we see how some nations have fought and obtained territory by cruel and horrible means. Sometimes it is out of greed and strife that their territories are enlarged. While humans believe that it is by their own strength and wisdom that they have acquired territory, behind it all is a sovereign God. Nothing could happen were it not for God. God's purposes are being worked out in the history of these nations.

He Wants Men to Know Him (verse 27)

This great and sovereign God wants to enter into a personal relationship with his creation. God wants people to reach out to him. This is difficult for us to understand. Why should such a great and awesome God want to relate to you and me? While we will never understand it, this is exactly what Paul is telling us here.

We Are His Offspring (verses 28–29)

We are God's offspring. He is our Father and we are his sons and daughters. The God of this universe has stamped his image on our lives. He has created us to enter into a personal relationship with him and delights to share his inheritance with us. Paul's God is a very personal God.

He Commands People Everywhere to Repent (verse 30)

This great and awesome God commands all people everywhere to repent. In the past he left people in their darkness. The Athenians were an example of this. God's primary concern was the nation of Israel. But through Christ he has extended his offer to all people everywhere. Every tribe and nation of earth is called on to repent and bow down to this one true God.

He Has Set a Date to Judge the World (verse 31)

God has set a day for judgment. He sent the Lord Jesus to earth to offer us forgiveness of sin. Jesus died on our behalf so that forgiveness could be possible, and he rose from the dead in the presence of many witnesses as proof that God had accepted his sacrifice. The day is coming when all who reject the Lord Jesus Christ will be judged and held accountable to God.

Notice the response to Paul's message. Some could not understand Paul's doctrine of the resurrection of the dead. The Epicureans believed that death was undisturbed sleep. They did not want to believe that their peaceful sleep would be disrupted. Others sneered at what Paul said, totally rejecting it. Still others remained open and wanted to hear more at another time. A few, however, accepted the message and believed in the name of the Lord Jesus. Among those who believed was a member of the Areopagus, a woman by the name of Damaris, and a number of others.

What was striking about Paul's stay in Athens was that the Athenians were quite open to listening to what Paul had to say. Paul was not stoned. He was not driven from their town. In spite of this, however, this city was the most resistant to the message of the gospel. While the Athenians were willing to listen, they were, for the most part, indifferent to what Paul said. Their intellectualism closed the door to the message of the gospel. It was not necessary for Satan to stir up the crowd against Paul. Here in Athens Satan simply used local intellectuals and pagan philosophies to scoff at what Paul had to say. The fact of the matter, however, is that humans do not determine what is true. The fact that these Greeks did not understand what Paul was saying did not change the fact that it was the truth and that one day they would be accountable to God for their rejection of it. You may not understand God and his Word, but it remains true. The unbelieving Athenians would perish in their religious intellectualism.

How our society needs to hear this message today. Many people use their emotions to try to determine right from wrong. How often we have seen people reject the truth of the Word of God for clever arguments based on human reason. This was the downfall of the Athenians.

For Consideration:

- What do you learn here about the extent of the sovereignty of God? What encouragement do you take from this?

- How much of a problem is intellectualism today? Does it keep people from accepting the truth? Explain.

- What will it take to break through to the intellectual who is resistant to the truth of the Word of God?

- What do we learn here about the personal nature of God?

For Prayer:

- Praise God for his sovereignty. Thank him that he is in absolute control of every situation in life.

- Praise God that though he is sovereign, he still wants to have a personal relationship with us.

- Do you have a friend or loved one who scoffs like the Athenians at faith in Christ? Take a moment to pray for him or her.

32

Paul's Second Missionary Journey

Part 6: Corinth

Read Acts 18:1–23

From Athens the apostle Paul traveled westward to the city of Corinth. There he met a Jew named Aquila who was from the region of Pontus in Italy. Aquila and his wife, Priscilla, had left Italy because of the declaration of Claudius the governor that forced all Jews out of Rome. This couple had left their home and business to seek out a new life as tentmakers in the city of Corinth. Because Paul was also a tentmaker, he stayed and worked with Aquila and Priscilla. We are not told that they were believers at this point. Could it be that they came to know the Lord as a result of the ministry of Paul?

Each Sabbath Paul would go to the synagogue, seeking to persuade those who came to worship that Jesus was their Messiah. When Silas and Timothy came from Macedonia to meet him as he had requested, Paul devoted himself entirely to the preaching of the good news of Christ. The question needs to be asked: What was it about the coming of

Timothy and Silas that enabled Paul to stop his tentmaking and devote himself to preaching? To answer this we need to look at two of Paul's letters. From 2 Corinthians 11:9 we read: "And when I was with you and needed something, I was not a burden to anyone, for the brothers who came from Macedonia supplied what I needed." In Philippians 4:15 we read: "Moreover, as you Philippians know, in the early days of your acquaintance with the gospel, when I set out from Macedonia, not one church shared with me in the matter of giving and receiving, except you only."

From these verses we understand that when Silas and Timothy arrived in Corinth, they had a gift of money for Paul from the churches in Macedonia. This gift enabled Paul to devote himself full-time to the preaching of the gospel. We see here how the Lord provided for Paul. Sometimes the Lord required that Paul work with his hands to provide for his own basic needs. At other times God moved the churches to give Paul financial aid. From this we see that Paul's walk of faith was not always a simple matter of sitting back and letting God provide. Sometimes God's provision came in the form of personal physical work.

It was not long before the Jews in Corinth took offence at the preaching of the gospel and became abusive toward Paul. Seeing their response, Paul "shook out his clothes" as a sign of protest against them and shifted his focus to the Gentiles in the region (verse 6). He left the synagogue and went to the home of a Gentile by the name of Titius Justus.

Paul's time in Corinth did produce fruit. Crispus, the synagogue ruler, believed in the Lord Jesus, as well as his entire family. Many Corinthian Gentiles came to know the Lord and were baptized as a sign of their identification with the Lord Jesus.

The growth of the church in Corinth did not please the Jews. Their abuse may have been a concern for Paul, but God spoke to him and encouraged him to persevere in his ministry there in Corinth. God promised to protect him from harm. There was still a great work for him to do in this city. With this encouragement Paul stayed for a year and a half, teaching the Word of God.

While God had promised to protect Paul, he had not promised the absence of trouble. The Jews attacked Paul and brought him to a Roman court. They charged him with "persuading the people to worship God in ways contrary to the law" (verse 13). Gallio, the proconsul, listened to the accusations of the Jews against Paul and then had the Jews ejected from court, saying that the matter really did not concern Roman law. Gallio told them to judge the case themselves.

Gallio's decision did not please the people. They turned on Sosthenes, the synagogue ruler, and beat him in front of the court. Gallio showed no concern whatsoever. Why would the Jews turn on Sosthenes, the ruler of the synagogue, when the accusations were against Paul? Could it be that Sosthenes, like Crispus the other ruler of the synagogue mentioned in verse 8, was sympathetic to Paul and his message? 1 Corinthians 1:1 tells us that the letter to the Corinthians was written by Paul and Sosthenes. It could be then that the Jews attacked Sosthenes because they saw him as a traitor to their cause.

After this event Paul stayed in Corinth for some time. He then left for Syria, accompanied by his friends Aquila and Priscilla. Paul had his head shaved because of a vow he had taken. This may have been a Nazarite vow. Numbers 6 tells us that an individual could make a special vow of separation to the Lord. Those taking this particular vow were not to cut their hair, drink wine, or go near a dead body (Numbers 6:3–6). Both Samson and Samuel had made these vows in the Old Testament times (Judges 13:7; 16:17 and 1 Samuel 1:11). When the vow was fulfilled, those taking the vow would shave their head and bring the hair to the temple in Jerusalem where it would be burned before the Lord (Numbers 6:18).

It is interesting to note that when Paul arrived in Jerusalem after his third missionary journey, the church encouraged him to join with some other believers in a purification rite that also involved the shaving of heads (Acts 21:24). This would lead us to believe that Paul was certainly not against taking such Old Testament vows.

From Corinth Paul and his companions traveled to Ephesus. Here again, Paul went into the synagogue and reasoned with the Jews. They asked Paul to stay with them for some time, but Paul refused, saying that he hoped to return another time to visit them. He was in a hurry to get home. This may have had something to do with his vow.

From Ephesus Paul traveled to Caesarea, just north of Jerusalem. Verse 22 tells us that from Caesarea he went up to visit the church. This very likely refers to the church in Jerusalem. Very often in Scripture, people are portrayed as "going up" to Jerusalem. This has to do with the fact that Jerusalem is located on a hill. It is possible that while he was in Jerusalem, he fulfilled his vow to the Lord. From Jerusalem Paul then returned to Antioch, the starting point of his second missionary journey. This ends the second missionary journey of Paul. We are not told if Timothy and Silas returned with Paul on this journey. It is possible that they remained behind to continue the work in Paul's absence.

During the course of this second missionary journey, many people had been touched with the gospel. Paul revisited the believers he had met on his first missionary journey with Barnabas. Churches were planted in Philippi, Thessalonica, and Corinth. We also have a record of believers in the cities of Berea and Ephesus. During the course of this trip, Paul had been cast into jail in Philippi, brought to trial in Corinth, and chased out of Thessalonica and Berea. Despite these inconveniences the work of God progressed. God's hand of protection was on Paul and kept him from harm. God had also provided for him financially throughout this entire mission.

For Consideration:

- Did Paul exercise faith in God when he worked as a tentmaker for his spending money?

- What evidence is there of the blessing of God on this second missionary journey of Paul? What evidence of God's blessing do you see on your own church?

- Was Paul against the laws of the Old Testament? What evidence for this do we see in this chapter?

For Prayer:

- Thank the Lord for the way he provides for your basic needs.

- Ask the Lord to raise up in our day more individuals like Paul.

- Ask God to make clear his calling on your life.

- Ask God to give you the discipline and perseverance of Paul.

33

Paul's Third Missionary Journey

Part 1: Apollos and John's Disciples

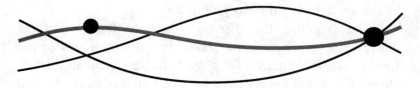

Read Acts 18:24–19:20

T he Apostle Paul had completed his second missionary journey. As he departed from cities where he had established churches, the Lord raised up other people to help in the preaching of the Word of God. One such individual was a very godly man by the name of Apollos, who demonstrated a real knowledge of the Word of God and was able to preach with authority and fervor. While Apollos understood who Jesus was, our passage tells us that he only knew the baptism of John. This appears to have been a real hindrance to him in his ministry.

When Aquila and Priscilla heard Apollos speak in Ephesus, they saw the potential in this man for the ministry of the gospel. They also saw gaps in his understanding, so they took him aside and explained to him more fully the way of God. Verses 27 and 28 tell us that when Apollos left Ephesus to go to his next preaching engagement, he was very useful to the brothers and sisters he met. He had a new power in his preaching and was able to prove from the Scriptures that Jesus was the Christ.

What was it that Aquila and Priscilla told Apollos that made such a difference in his life? The passage does not say. Verse 25, however, states that he only knew the baptism of John. When Paul arrived in the city of Ephesus on his third missionary journey, he met some disciples of John the Baptist (19:1). It appears that these disciples had the same problem as Apollos. Paul asked them if they had received the Holy Spirit when they believed. They told Paul that they had never heard of the Holy Spirit.

Like Apollos, the disciples did not have complete understanding. There is no doubt that they believed in the Lord Jesus. Their master John had been very clear about this. He preached that Jesus Christ was the Lamb of God who had come to take away the sins of the world (John 1:29). While these individuals seemed to understand these facts, they had never personally experienced the empowering work of the Holy Spirit in their lives. They had more or less the right beliefs but, like Apollos, they had no real life and power.

We are not told what Paul said to these disciples. What we do know, however, is that Paul spoke to them about Jesus whom John the Baptist proclaimed. The result of Paul's teaching was that these disciples turned their hearts and lives over to Jesus and identified with him in baptism. When Paul laid his hands on them, they also received the Holy Spirit and showed evidences of his presence by speaking in tongues and prophesying. Could it be that Apollos had the same problem? He knew about the Lord Jesus and yet lacked understanding of the power of the Holy Spirit in his life. None of these men would be the same after experiencing the reality of the Holy Spirit's work in their lives.

This indwelling and empowering of the Holy Spirit made all the difference in the lives of these individuals. Apollos knew and preached the truth about Christ but did not understand the need of the Holy Spirit. The disciples of John the Baptist were trying to serve the Lord in their own strength and wisdom. The work to which God has called us is not done in human effort and wisdom. We desperately need the empowering work of the Holy Spirit in our lives. He wants to empower and anoint us in ministry, but we have all too often failed to understand our need of him. Could it be that we too, like Apollos and the disciples of John the Baptist, need to experience a fresh work of the Holy Spirit in our lives and ministries?

After speaking with these disciples, Paul went to the synagogue in Ephesus. For three months Paul spoke boldly in the name of the Lord Jesus. Despite the fact that Paul was a man filled with the Spirit of God, there were those who remained obstinate. Their hearts were indifferent to the powerful and clear teaching of the Word of God. Some of these individuals publicly ridiculed Paul's teaching. Because they rejected his message, Paul left the synagogue and moved to a lecture hall in the town. There he met daily with all who wanted to listen. He stayed in Ephesus for two years, teaching and preaching the Word of God.

During those two years, the city of Ephesus saw a very visible demonstration of the power of God's Spirit. Extraordinary miracles were performed as the Spirit of God moved powerfully through the life of Paul. So powerfully that even handkerchiefs and aprons that touched him were taken to the sick and they were healed. People were physically healed of their diseases in the name of the Lord Jesus. Demons were cast out of those who were possessed. Through these powerful signs, God was confirming his presence and the truth of the message that Paul preached. Ephesus was being greatly impacted by the power of God at work in the apostle Paul.

We need to understand that this passage is not intended to be a manual on how God wants to work in us today. God is able to heal in any way he chooses. There are no records of people touching the Lord with handkerchiefs and then using them to heal others. This is how God worked in Paul. He worked in the life of the Lord Jesus in a different way. We should never attempt to reduce the work of God to a set of rules and procedures. Nor should we try to imitate what God does in others. What is important is that we be obedient to his leading and remain under the authority of his Word.

Some itinerant Jewish exorcists were impressed by what they were seeing around them. Observing how Paul cast out demons, these exorcists decided that they were going to do the same. They would invoke the name of the Lord Jesus over those who were possessed by evil spirits, commanding them to leave in the name of the Lord Jesus whom Paul preached. It is hard to imagine the Jews, who were such bitter enemies of the Christians, ever invoking the name of the Lord Jesus, but they could not deny the evidence they saw around them. While these people were not willing to yield their lives to the Lord Jesus, they were forced to recognize that there was great power in his name. It's surprising how close we can come to the Lord Jesus without ever accepting him. These Jews recognized that the name of Jesus was a powerful name. They saw what was happening in his name. They even ministered in his name, but they had never bowed the knee to him.

Notice what happened to these exorcists who were using the name of the Lord Jesus. Verse 15 tells us that one day when they spoke to a demon and commanded it to leave in the name of Jesus, the man he possessed jumped on these seven exorcists and beat them up. They ran from the house naked, beaten, and bleeding.

Matthew 7:22–23 tells us that in the last days there will be those who never knew the Lord but who cast out demons in the his name. We should not assume, therefore, that the reason these individuals failed was because they did not know the Lord (even though we could present a powerful argument to this effect). What we need to understand from this passage, however, is that the name of the Lord is not a magical formula that we can recite in order to get our heart's desire. The Lord's name is to be honored and respected. The ministry of spiritual warfare is not something to be taken lightly.

Notice the response of the people of Ephesus to what had happened to these seven Jewish exorcists. A great fear overcame the inhabitants of the city and the name of the Lord was held in "high honor" (see verse 17). They knew that the only power bigger than that of the evil spirits was the power of God.

God used the defeat of the seven sons of Sceva to accomplish a great work in the city. Amazed by the evil power of demons and by the even greater power of the Lord Jesus, men and women came to accept the Lord Jesus. Many who had practiced sorcery brought their religious scrolls and cast them in a great pile for public burning. This was nothing short of a great revival in the city of Ephesus. It was estimated that the value of the demonic material burned in the city that day was fifty thousand drachmas. One drachma was the equivalent of a day's work. The amount of demonic material burned that day was the equivalent of 160 years of work. In other words, it would take three people working over six days a week for fifty-three years to pay for the material burned that day. God was truly working in the city of Ephesus.

We see from this section that there was a lack of power in some of the early disciples who ministered in Ephesus. Paul, Aquila, and Priscilla were used of God to point the believers there to the power of the Holy Spirit. Through the apostle Paul, God showed the Ephesians what his Spirit could do. Revival began to sweep through the city of Ephesus. The whole city was astonished by God and the evidence of his presence. People bowed the knee to the Lord Jesus for the first time. For others it meant coming to grips with their sin. We see here in this city a very powerful demonstration of victory over the enemy in the public burning of demonic material. What began in the life of Apollos and the disciples of John the Baptist spilled over into the rest of the community. May the Holy Spirit do that work in us also.

For Consideration:

• Compare the powerless faith of the disciples of John with what they saw God doing in the ministry of the apostle Paul. How does the church today compare with these two examples?

• Why do we not see this power today?

• What is the difference between serving the Lord in our own strength and serving the Lord in the power of the Holy Spirit?

• What role does the Holy Spirit have today?

For Prayer:

• Pray that God would move in revival in your town.

• Ask him to show you what is lacking in your faith.

• Ask God to forgive you for believing that you can serve him without the empowering ministry of the Holy Spirit.

• Ask God to teach you to hear and follow the leading of the Spirit of God.

34

Paul's Third Missionary Journey

Part 2: Demetrius

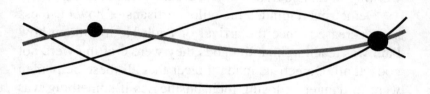

Read Acts 19:21–41

I n the last meditation we saw how God had been ministering through the apostle Paul in Ephesus and bringing about nothing short of a great revival. Verses 21 and 22 tell us that after leaving Ephesus, Paul would go to Jerusalem through the region of Macedonia and Achaia where he had ministered on his second missionary journey. Timothy and Erastus would accompany him on this journey in the region of Macedonia. Verses 23 to the end of this chapter seem to take us back in time to the events that surrounded Paul's departure from Ephesus. Let us look at these events in some detail.

As we have already seen, the Lord had ministered powerfully in Ephesus. The city had experienced a public burning of demonic material. Things were radically changing for the good. This change, however, did not meet with the approval of all the citizens of Ephesus. In particular, a man by the name of Demetrius objected to Paul and his influence. Demetrius made his living by making shrines to the goddess Artemis. In fact, many of the artisans of Ephesus made a great profit from these religious artifacts. Ephesus was a major center for the worship of the goddess Artemis. Since the arrival of Paul in Ephesus, however, sales of these religious articles had gone down. People were no longer worshiping Artemis as they once had. The artisans were losing money. Demetrius felt that something needed to be done. He called a meeting of all the craftsmen and those working in related trades to discuss the issue at hand.

Demetrius reminded his fellow artisans of how business had decreased since the arrival of Paul. He told them how Paul was teaching that the gods they were crafting were not gods at all. Demetrius made it clear that all these craftsmen were in danger of losing their businesses if something was not done about Paul. Demetrius also appealed to religious pride by showing his fellow tradesmen that the name of Artemis would soon be discredited and robbed of her "divine majesty" (verse 27). Ephesus was known for its temple to the honor of Artemis. This great temple, according to Demetrius, would be dishonored.

Demetrius was successful in riling these artisans. They begin to angrily cry out: "Great is Artemis of the Ephesians!" (verse 28). From that little group, the outcry spread to the whole city and caused a riot. The crowd seized Gaius and Aristarchus, some traveling companions of the apostle Paul, and brought them into the theater. We are not told what the furious crowd intended to do to them.

In verse 22 we read that Timothy and Erastus were Paul's helpers on this missionary journey. Verse 29 tells us that Gaius and Aristarchus were also his traveling companions. It is interesting to see how this group is expanding. On the first missionary journey, Paul and Barnabas seem to have been traveling alone. On the second missionary journey, we have the record of Paul, Timothy, and Silas traveling together.

Now on the third journey, we have the record of Paul and four other missionaries traveling together. It appears that more and more people were getting involved in missions.

The crowd had brought Aristarchus and Gaius by force to the theater. Paul wanted to go to the theater and speak to the mob, but the local believers refused to allow him to do this. Very likely they were trying to save Paul's life. Even some of the city officials who were Paul's friends begged Paul not to go to the theater. His presence would only serve to make things worse. There are times when all we can do is to place our problems in the Lord's hands and leave them there. Sometimes our involvement only makes matters worse.

The mob that had gathered was in a state of total confusion. Some people shouted one thing, some another. Verse 32 tells us that many people did not even know why they were there. The Jews pushed to the front a man by the name of Alexander and shouted some instructions to him. He motioned for silence and was about to speak in defense of his people. When the crowd realized, however, that he was a Jew, they began to shout: "Great is Artemis of the Ephesians" (verse 34). This continued for another two hours.

A question may be legitimately asked: Why did the Jews push Alexander to the front? Verse 33 tells us that he was going to make a defense for his people, the Jews. Why did the Jews need someone to come to their defense? The crowd had gathered to protest Paul and his message. The Jews would have been happy to join this protest. They did not like him any more than did the devotees of Artemis. It seems that there must have been some confusion in the minds of the worshipers of Artemis about the difference between the Christians and the Jews. It is quite likely that the Ephesians viewed Christians and Jews as being the same. It would have been easy for pagans to confuse these two groups. Paul had spoken in the synagogue. He had spoken about the Jewish

Scriptures and the Messiah. Besides this, the worshipers of Artemis knew that the Jews also refused to bow the knee to Artemis, and at this point, they resented anyone who did not worship her.

The next person to stand up before the crowd was the city clerk. He at least was able to quiet the crowd. He reminded them that no one could deny that Ephesus was the great guardian of the temple of Artemis and her image, which they believed had fallen from heaven. No one could take these facts from them. Their outrage, however, did not accomplish anything. He encouraged the artisans of the town to go through the proper channels. They were free to take this matter to court. As it was, the crowd had brought Gaius and Aristarchus to trial although they had done nothing wrong, and under Roman law the whole city was guilty of rioting. If the rioting did not stop, the city would have to give an account to the Roman officials for these activities. Because everyone feared the authority of Rome, they decided to take the city clerk's advice. With this, the crowd broke up and went home.

We see here how God protected his people. Aristarchus and Gaius could have been seriously harmed, but God protected them. Paul himself could have been killed, but the Lord had kept Paul away from the angry mob. God had not finished with Paul. As a sovereign God, he would hedge Paul in so that no one could harm him before his ministry was complete. There was no safer place for Paul to be than in the will of God. Even though everything around him seemed to be falling apart, inside the circle of God's will there was absolute peace and security. This ought to encourage us in our walk with the Lord.

There is a second thing we need to notice here in this account. Paul wanted to go to the theater. Obviously, his intentions were to help calm the situation and protect his traveling companions. Paul did not want to sit idly by and watch the crowd harm or possibly kill his friends. The fact of the matter, however, was that the presence of Paul could have precipitated his companions' deaths by increasing the mob's rage. The local disciples knew this and advised Paul to stay away from the theater. Paul took their advice. The Lord proved that he was big enough to handle the situation without Paul. In fact, God's way was perfect.

There are times when you and I will have to sit back and give our problems to the Lord. Sometimes there is absolutely nothing we can do. In these situations we can be assured of one thing. God is big enough to take care of our problems by himself. He can accomplish his purposes perfectly well without us. Paul realized the value of the advice of his friends. He had the humility to submit and confess that his plan was not good. This whole situation, however, showed Paul that it was time for him to move on. God had made his plan for Paul very clear.

While this situation had the makings of being very tragic, God worked it all out. He can do the same for us in the difficulties we find ourselves in today. His ways are perfect. Even though you may feel helpless, God is big enough to work it all out. He will not let you down.

For Consideration:

- Have you ever felt that you needed to take control of life's situations? Why is it so hard to let go and let God take care of these situations?

- How do we know when we should let go of a situation and leave it with God, instead of trying to take care of it ourselves?

- What do we learn here about the protection of God on his chosen servants?

- Is God obliged to use only believers to accomplish his purposes? Who does God use to disperse the mob and rescue his people? What does this teach us about the people that God is able to use?

For Prayer:

- Thank God that he is big enough to care for every need you have.

- Ask him to quiet your heart and enable you to rest in him.

- Thank the Lord for his protection on your life.

- Thank him that he is able to use even the unbeliever to accomplish his purposes.

- Ask God to give you courage and boldness to face the trials that have come your way.

35

Paul's Third Missionary Journey

Part 3: Macedonia and Miletus

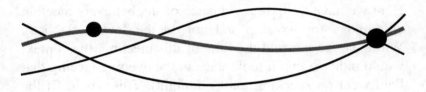

Read Acts 20:1–38

After the riot in Ephesus, Paul spent time encouraging the believers there and then left for the Roman colony of Macedonia. Paul traveled through Macedonia, encouraging the believers on the way, and when he reached Greece, he stayed for three months. His intentions were to sail from Greece to Antioch in Syria. These plans changed, however, when a plot against him was discovered. Paul decided instead to go back by land through Macedonia.

As Paul traveled through Macedonia, he was accompanied by at least seven men: Sopater from the town of Berea, Aristarchus and Secondus from Thessalonica, Gaius from Derbe, Timothy from Lystra, and Tychicus and Trophimus from the province of Asia. These men went to Troas by land while Paul remained in Philippi for the Feast of Unleavened Bread. Paul then sailed from Philippi to Troas, where he met them. Verse 5 leads us to believe that

Paul did not go alone to Troas. This would indicate that there were more than seven in this band of traveling missionaries. It is quite possible that Paul could have been accompanied by Luke the writer of the book of Acts. The whole team remained in Troas for a week.

While the missionary team was in Troas, the believers gathered together to break bread. There is much evidence in Scripture that the Lord's Supper was observed on a weekly basis in the early church. Notice that these believers were gathering on the first day of the week and not the seventh. Here we have Scriptural evidence of the believers meeting on Sunday for worship and not on the Jewish Sabbath. While we are not told the time of this meeting, the context would indicate that it took place in the evening (seeing that Paul went on speaking until midnight). This would fit the historical context as well. The first day of the week was a regular workday. It would not be until the reign of Emperor Constantine that Sunday would be recognized as a religious holiday. It is very likely that these early believers worked on Sunday during the day and gathered on Sunday evening for worship.

Seated in a window was a man by the name of Eutychus. Obviously, things in the early church were somewhat informal. Not too many people coming into our modern churches would have the freedom to sit up on a window ledge to listen to the preacher. As Paul spoke, Eutychus fell into a deep sleep and fell from the window ledge to the ground below. When people went down to pick him up, they discovered that he was dead. Paul threw himself on the man and placed his arms around him. Eutychus was restored to life. Then everyone returned to the room upstairs, broke bread, had fellowship, and listened to Paul preach until daylight. When daybreak came, Paul left them. We can only admire the devotion of this group of believers who were willing to stay all night to hear the Word of God.

From Troas Paul's companions boarded a ship and sailed southward to Assos. Paul decided to go by land from Troas and meet them in Assos. We are not told why Paul refused to board the ship at this point. We can be sure, however, that these moments of solitude were spent in communion with the Lord. When Paul met his traveling companions in Assos, he boarded the ship and sailed to Miletus after a series of short stops.

Since Paul was in a hurry to get to Jerusalem for Pentecost, he decided not to stop in Ephesus. Instead, he chose to stop at the port city of Miletus and call for the elders of the church in Ephesus to come and meet him there. When the elders arrived, Paul reminded them of his faithful service over the years in the city of Ephesus. Paul also told the elders about his plans to go to Jerusalem. He revealed to them his uncertainty about his trip to Jerusalem. The Holy Spirit had told him that prison and hardships awaited him there in that city. Paul's conviction that he needed to go to Jerusalem, however, was stronger than his fear of what the Jews might do to him there. Paul told the elders that this would probably be the last time they would ever see him. He was leaving them, however, with a clear conscience. He had faithfully preached the gospel to them. He was innocent of their blood. He had left nothing unsaid that ought to have been said. I wonder if we could say the same thing today? Are we free of the blood of people? How often have we fallen short and left unsaid those things that ought to be said in the cause of the gospel? As Paul left the Ephesian elders, he had a clear conscience before God. He had done everything the Lord had asked him to do. If only we could live with such a conscience ourselves.

In verses 28–31 Paul gave a charge to the elders of Ephesus. He challenged them first to keep watch as shepherds over the flock that God had entrusted into their care. In verse 28 he reminded these leaders that their commission was divine. The Holy Spirit himself had gifted and called these particular men to be the leaders and shepherds of God's people in Ephesus. Paul warned these elders that the day was coming when wolves would seek to infiltrate the flock and to draw people away from the truth of the Word of God. Revelation 2:1–7 reminds us that the Ephesians did struggle with these wolves. The Nicolaitans infiltrated their community, teaching false doctrine. In addition, there were false teachers claiming to be apostles in their midst. Paul's prophecy did come true.

Paul gave these elders his own example to follow. When he was with them, he never ceased to watch out for them and care for them in their need. He warned them day and night with tears streaming down his cheeks. He challenged the elders to do the same. What a challenge this is to the elders and deacons of our present churches. If you are an elder or deacon, has your heart been broken for God's people? The task that God has entrusted to you cannot be taken lightly.

Second, Paul commended these elders to God and to his Word. This Word could build them up and give them an inheritance among those who were sanctified. This meant that these elders had to be men of the Word. It was the Word of God that would guide and direct them in the way they should live. By carefully following the principles of the Word of God, they could become everything that God meant them to be. They were to be guided by the principles of this Word as they served the church. Only by obedience to this Word could the church in Ephesus become everything that God meant it to be. Paul challenged the elders to be first and foremost men of the Word.

Finally, Paul warned the elders against the temptation of seeing their ministry as a means to financial and material gain. Paul reminded them of how he himself had lived among them. Never had he coveted what others had. He had not sought any financial remuneration from them in his ministry. Paul had worked hard to provide for his own basic needs. He had done this to show the church that it was more blessed to give than to receive. If these elders were going to be everything that God meant them to be, they would have to be willing to exercise their ministry in self-sacrificing ways.

In Paul's writings he tells us that laborers are worthy of their hire. Paul teaches us that it is acceptable to gain one's livelihood from the gospel (1 Timothy 5:17; 1 Corinthians 9:11–14). What he is saying here in this passage, however, is that this should never be the motivation behind the ministry. In our day it is not uncommon to see pastors accepting or refusing a position purely because of prestige and financial considerations. While these Christian workers needed to be provided for, money was never to be the motivation behind their ministry.

While money is the focus of this particular passage, there are other temptations for the elder or pastor. It is possible to desire the office of elder or pastor in order to gain respect. There are many reasons why an individual could seek office in a church. Paul challenged the elders of Ephesus not to seek office for selfish reasons. The only motive for ministry ought to be the glory of God.

After giving the leaders this charge, Paul knelt down with them and prayed, very likely committing each other to the Lord's care. This parting was particularly difficult because they knew that some of them would never see Paul again. From this moment on, Paul's freedom would be limited. His next missionary journey would be in chains. He boldly faced this prospect, knowing that it was the will of God for him. I wonder if we would have the same courage.

For Consideration:

- Could you say that you have lived with a clear conscience over the last year? Are there things you have left unsaid or undone?

- Consider Paul's threefold challenge to the Ephesian elders. What particularly stands out for you in this challenge?

- What is the central motivation in your personal ministry?

- Would you be willing to serve the Lord even if it meant serious persecution and difficulties?

For Prayer:

- Confess any shortcomings that have kept you from living with a clear conscience before God.

- Ask the Lord to help you live with a clear conscience before him.

- Pray for the spiritual leadership of your church using Paul's threefold challenge as a guide.

36

Jerusalem

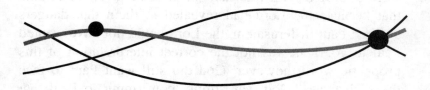

Read Acts 21:1–36

I t was not easy for Paul and his companions to tear themselves away from the Ephesian elders. This parting was very difficult. From Miletus, where they had met with the elders, Paul's missionary team sailed southward past the cities of Cos, Rhodes, and Patara. From Patara they boarded a ship heading toward Phoenicia. The ship sailed past Cyprus and arrived in the port city of Tyre.

In Tyre Paul and his companions met with some believers and stayed with them seven days. During this time these believers warned Paul not to go to Jerusalem. Verse 4 tells us that it was "through the Spirit" that Paul was warned not to go up to Jerusalem. Verse 5, however, tells us that Paul went anyway. This causes us to wonder if Paul was being disobedient. It is clear that Paul knew that his time was coming to an end. The Spirit of God had revealed to him that the road to Jerusalem was filled with many difficulties and trials. This word from the Lord was confirmed in Tyre.

The believers there had the distinct impression that the Lord was telling them that Paul would suffer in Jerusalem. Having received this word from the Lord, the believers, not wanting to lose Paul, very likely took it on themselves to discourage him from going to Jerusalem. Paul, on the other hand, was not afraid of the difficulties he would encounter. He felt that the Lord was leading him to Jerusalem and refused to be discouraged in what he believed to be the will of the Lord.

We see in this situation the danger of trying to interpret a word of prophecy. It was easy for these believers to assume that because the Lord had revealed to them that dangers awaited Paul in Jerusalem, the Lord could not have wanted Paul to go. This was not the correct interpretation of this prophetic word, however. God did still want Paul to face these obstacles. God was simply confirming to Paul that there would be trials awaiting him.

Paul and his companions took leave of the believers after a time of prayer on the beach. From Tyre they traveled to Ptolemais where they greeted the local Christians and stayed for a day. The next day they arrived in Caesarea where they stayed in the home of Philip the evangelist who was one of the seven deacons chosen by the church of Jerusalem. He had four unmarried daughters who had the gift of prophecy.

While Paul was in Caesarea, a prophet by the name of Agabus arrived from the region of Judea. He took Paul's belt and tied his own hands and feet with it, telling Paul that this is what would happen to him in Jerusalem. Agabus warned Paul that he would be handed over to the Gentiles. When the believers heard this, they sought to discourage Paul from going to Jerusalem. This was the second group of believers who had received this word from the Lord. Paul himself had received this same word. There could be no doubt that this was very definitely from the Lord. Once again, Paul refused to give in to the wishes of the believers. He told them very clearly that he was not only willing to be bound but also to die for the name of the Lord Jesus. When they saw that he would not be dissuaded in this matter, they committed him to the will of God and sent him off to Jerusalem, accompanied by several brothers. They all stayed with a fellow believer by the name of Mnason, an early convert from the region of Cyprus.

As we think about the repetition of this warning to Paul about the dangers that awaited him in Jerusalem, we cannot help but see that the Lord wanted Paul to know what was about to happen. Could it be that the Lord wanted to prepare Paul for the next stage of his life? Why did God tell these things to Paul? He certainly did not tell them to him so that he could run away from the coming struggles. The Lord informed Paul in order to prepare him. When these trials finally came, they did not take Paul by surprise. Because God had made it so clear to him, Paul would have seen these trials as the outworking of God's purposes in his life. His sufferings would have built him up in the faith and not discouraged him.

The fulfillment of this prophecy did not take long to be realized. When Paul arrived in Jerusalem, the brothers warmly received him. Paul met with James, the leader of the Jerusalem church, and with the other elders. The elders gave Paul the opportunity to share the great work of God that was taking place among the Gentiles. This was tremendous news for the church in Jerusalem, but it brought up an issue that needed to be dealt with very quickly. The church informed Paul that not everyone was happy with his ministry. There were thousands of Jews who where spreading stories that Paul was teaching the Gentiles to turn away from Moses and the Law. This situation had the potential of being very dangerous. The church felt that something needed to be done right away to calm these anxious Jews.

In the Jerusalem church four men had made a particular vow to the Lord. This vow could quite possibly have been a

Jewish Nazarite vow. Persons taking this vow of separation would not cut their hair, eat or drink any fruit of the vine, or touch any dead body. When the time of their vow had ended, they would go to the temple and have their head shaved. The hair was offered to the Lord as a sacrifice. They would then go through a period of purification after which they would be freed from their vow. The church encouraged Paul to take part in this ceremony. They asked him to pay the expenses of these four men as a sign that the reports the Jews were circulating about him were unfounded. Paul agreed to the plan and the next day he went with the men to the temple to begin the period of purification.

What was intended to be a means of reconciling the differences between Paul and the Jews actually served to widen the gap between them. When the days of purification were almost ended, some Jews from Asia came into the temple and saw Paul there with these four men. They spread the story that Paul had gone into the temple with Gentiles and had defiled the house of God. This merited, according to Jewish law, the strictest of punishments. If found guilty of this crime, Paul would have been put to death. While this story was unfounded, it did serve to rile the Jewish population who already hated Paul. Jews came to the temple and dragged Paul out. As they were trying to kill him, news of what was happening reached the commander of the Roman troops. He immediately sent his soldiers to stop the riot and restore order. Paul narrowly avoided death. Instead, he was bound in chains and held in custody by the Roman soldiers.

When the commander asked the crowd why they were trying to kill Paul, some shouted one thing and some another. The commander could not get to the truth. He decided to take Paul away and keep him in the barracks. This did not please the mob. The Bible tells us that they became so violent that when Paul reached the steps, he had to be carried by the soldiers to avoid being beaten by the crowd. The mob followed Paul, crying out for his death.

Things were not going to be easy for the apostle Paul. He refused to give up, however. He was willing to face the falsehoods and angry shouts of the crowd. He was willing to be beaten, bound, and even killed for the sake of the Lord Jesus. He had had every opportunity to avoid this occurrence. He had been warned and encouraged by believers to avoid the trials and struggles that surely awaited him in Jerusalem. But Paul chose to directly face what the Lord had for him. Paul would not be distracted. He wanted God's perfect will for his life, and he was willing to pay the ultimate price.

For Consideration:

• Have you ever found yourself taking the "easy road" instead of directly facing things? Give some examples of this.

• In this passage Paul chose not to listen to the church's counsel. What does this teach us about discerning the will of God? What role does the counsel of others play in our understanding of God's will?

For Prayer:

• Ask the Lord to give you courage to face your trials.

• Ask God to give you discernment to know his leading and to be able to distinguish his voice from all the other voices around you.

• Thank God for the way he has promised to be with you in your trials. Thank him for a particular time in your life when you experienced his hand in a moment of difficulty.

37

Paul's Trial

Part 1: His Defense before the Crowd

Read Acts 21:37–22:29

Paul began what would prove to be a very lengthy defense of his ministry. The remaining chapters of the book of Acts record Paul defending himself at least six times: before the people of Jerusalem, the Sanhedrin, Felix, Festus, Agrippa, and eventually Caesar himself. Let us look at the first of these defenses. Here Paul stood before the angry mob in Jerusalem.

Paul had just been arrested. The soldiers had to carry him to protect him from the angry crowd that sought his life. It seems that the whole city was against him. Despite this discouragement Paul wanted to speak to the crowd. He asked the commander if he could say a few words to the people. The commander was quite surprised to hear that Paul could speak Greek because he thought that Paul was an Egyptian terrorist who, some time before these events, had led four thousand terrorists in a revolt (see verse 38).

Realizing that Paul was not the Egyptian revolutionary,

the commander gave him permission to speak. The commander was no doubt interested to hear what Paul had to say in his defense, and, at least this way, he could make some sense of the events that were transpiring that day. Even the people in the angry mob were not agreed on what Paul was saying.

Having received permission to speak, Paul stood on the steps and motioned for the crowd to be silent. After he had addressed the commander in Greek, Paul then spoke in Aramaic to the Jews gathered before him that day. What is particularly interesting about this defense is the fact that Paul mentioned nothing about the misunderstanding that had started the riot. The commotion had erupted because of a misunderstanding about why Paul had been in the temple. If I had been Paul, I would have probably placed the emphasis on the fact that the whole thing was a misinterpretation of the facts. I would have probably told the crowd that I was not against the Law of Moses, as they claimed. Paul did not seem interested in speaking about these issues. His main concern here was to share with the crowd his testimony of salvation in the Lord Jesus.

Paul began his speech by informing the crowd about his past. He told them that he was a Jew born in Tarsus but brought up in Jerusalem. He had studied under one of the greatest and most influential Jewish teachers of his day, a man by the name of Gamaliel. In regard to his zeal for the Law of Moses, Paul reminded them that he had even gone to the extent of persecuting Christians, throwing them into prison and seeking their deaths. He reminded them that the High Priest and Jewish ruling council could testify to the fact that he had received letters of permission to go to Damascus to find followers of Jesus to bring them back to Jerusalem for trial. Paul had been the leader in the Jewish movement to rid the world of Christians.

Paul went on to explain that as he had been on his way to

Damascus, a bright light had shone from heaven and knocked him to the ground. He had heard a voice calling out to him: "Saul! Saul! Why do you persecute me?" (verse 7) Paul had not known who was speaking to him, so he had asked the person to identify himself. The voice had responded: "I am Jesus of Nazareth, whom you are persecuting" (verse 8). Paul's companions on the road to Damascus that day had been witnesses to the light, although they had not understood what the voice had been saying.

Paul told the crowd that after this encounter that he was no longer the same man. His meeting with the Lord Jesus had radically changed his life forever. Paul had asked the Lord that day: "What shall I do, Lord?" The Lord had told him to go into the city and wait for instructions. Paul's companions had led him into Damascus by the hand because he had been totally blinded by the light. The Lord Jesus had conquered him.

As Paul had waited in Damascus, a man by the name of Ananias had come to see him. Ananias was a very devout observer of the Law. Paul emphasized the fact that Ananias was respected by all the Jews in the area. Possibly, even these people in Jerusalem had heard about Ananias. It was through Ananias that Paul received his sight again. Ananias had received a word from the Lord for Paul and had informed him that God had chosen him to be a witness to the things he had seen and heard.

What were these things? Ananias had been referring to Paul's encounter with the Lord Jesus. There was no doubt in the mind of Paul that the Lord Jesus was very much alive. God had called Paul to testify to this fact. Ananias had then commanded Paul to take a step of identification with Christ and be baptized as a follower of the Lord Jesus in order to have his sins forgiven by calling on his name.

What a beautiful picture we have here. Paul was guilty before God for persecuting the church. Because of Paul many believers had lost their lives and others were beaten or imprisoned. Despite Paul's horrible crimes, God offered him forgiveness in the name of the Righteous One he had been persecuting. It does not matter what our pasts have been—there is forgiveness in the name of the Lord.

Paul continued telling his story to the crowd. He had left Damascus and returned to Jerusalem. In a vision God had revealed that he was to leave Jerusalem because the Jews would not accept his message. He was to go to the Gentiles and proclaim the message of forgiveness of sin through the Lord Jesus.

In this brief testimony, the apostle Paul had explained how he had come to know the Lord Jesus and how he had been called into ministry. His conscience was clear before God: he had been obedient to God's call on his life. The crowd listened to his testimony until he said that God had sent him to the Gentiles. At that point the crowd's anger flared again. "Rid the earth of him!" they cried (verse 22). With that, they began to pick up dust and throw it into the air, casting off their cloaks. These were obviously signs of contempt for Paul and his message.

Seeing what was taking place, the commander ordered that Paul be taken into the barracks, flogged, and questioned in order to find out why the people were shouting like this at him. As Paul was stretched out to be flogged, he asked if it was legal for them to beat a Roman citizen. When the commander discovered that Paul was born a citizen of Rome, he became alarmed. He did not have the right to beat a Roman citizen without giving him a proper trial. So Paul was spared the ill treatment.

While the hearts of the people of Jerusalem had not changed, God had given Paul the opportunity to proclaim Christ to those who had sought his death. Paul's main concern had been not so much to defend himself but rather to present Christ and the ministry that Christ had given him. God's presence had been with Paul in this trial. The crowd had unsuccessfully tried to kill him. The commander of the army had tried to flog him but, on learning of Paul's citizenship, refrained from doing so. I am convinced that Paul was very much aware of the presence of God at this moment of his life. I am sure that his heart was filled with the peace of God, knowing that nothing could happen to him that God did not intend. In this terrible moment in Paul's life, he committed himself to the Lord's care. Paul felt no need to take matters into his own hands. He did not speak in his own defense. God was his defender. Paul trusted God fully. May this be our experience as we face the obstacles that come our way.

For Consideration:

- Have you ever had moments when you felt compelled to defend your honor against false accusations? When is it necessary to stand up in our own defense, and when do we simply leave matters in the Lord's hands?

- Paul was not concerned here about what the people thought of him. He was more concerned about preaching the gospel. Explain how the desire to look good before others can ultimately be a snare for us in ministry.

- What encouragement do you find in the fact that the Lord Jesus wants to use you as a witness to those around you?

- What does this passage teach us about the protection of the Lord in the midst of trials and persecution?

For Prayer:

- Thank the Lord that even though others may not understand our motives, the Lord God knows our intentions.

- Ask the Lord to help you to be set free from what others think about you.

- Ask him to give you a greater boldness to stand up for him, as the apostle Paul did.

- Thank the Lord for his protection on your life.

38

Paul's Trial

Part 2: His Defense before the Sanhedrin

Read Acts 22:30–23:35

P aul had stood before the crowd and offered his defense. The commander of the army was still uncertain of Paul's crime, but he knew, however, that the crime was of some religious nature. This Roman official, therefore, called a meeting of the chief priests and the Jewish ruling council. While matters related to the Jewish religion did not directly concern the commander, the intensity of hatred for Paul was such that it demanded an explanation.

When the Sanhedrin and the chief priests had gathered, Paul was brought before them and asked to present his defense. Paul immediately got himself into trouble when he told the leaders that he had a good conscience before God. The chief priest could not believe that Paul would say such a thing because Paul had been ministering to the Gentiles as though they had an equal standing with the Jews before God. Paul had been accused of bringing Gentiles into the temple and had even claimed that the Messiah had come. How could

Paul possibly say that he had a good conscience before God? The chief priest ordered that Paul be struck in the mouth for his blasphemous and proud remarks. It was obvious that this council already had its mind made up about Paul.

Not knowing that it was the high priest who ordered him to be struck, Paul spoke out against him. Paul told the high priest that he was a hypocrite. When someone told Paul that the one to whom he spoke was the high priest, Paul admitted that he had made a mistake. We see the humility of Paul in this matter. He was not afraid to confess that he was wrong.

There is a challenge here for us. How careful we need to be about criticizing those whom God has placed in authority over us. It is true that we may not agree with what they are doing, but God commands us to be respectful of them because of their position. Paul recognized his sin (see Exodus 22:28) and confessed it. How often have we been guilty of speaking out against our political or religious leaders? May God help us to be respectful of his chosen servants.

Paul knew that the Sanhedrin was composed of both Pharisees and Sadducees. The Sadducees did not believe in the resurrection or in beings such as angels or spirits. The Pharisees, on the other hand, believed in both. Paul continued his defense before this mixed group. He informed them that he was a Pharisee and that he was on trial before them because of his hope in the resurrection of the dead. That statement threw the whole council into disorder. It set the Sadducees against the Pharisees in their age-old dispute concerning a resurrection. The Pharisees stood their ground in the belief in the resurrection and said: "We find nothing wrong with this man. . . . What if a spirit or an angel has spoken to him?" (verse 9). This statement did not go over well with the Sadducees. The dispute became heated. The commander, who had been listening to what was going on, realized that Paul would be torn to pieces if he remained in the meeting, so the commander ordered that Paul be taken back to the barracks.

In all this the presence of the Lord was again very much in evidence. God had protected Paul from the same council that had passed the death sentence on our Lord. God defended Paul by throwing his enemies into a state of confusion.

After these events the Lord appeared to Paul, telling him to take courage because he would testify in Rome, even as he had testified in Jerusalem. We get the distinct impression that the Lord was pleased with Paul and his faithfulness to testify to his name.

The next morning, considering that the Sanhedrin had been unsuccessful in dealing with Paul, some of the Jews banded together and swore an oath that they would neither eat nor drink until they had killed Paul. There were over forty men involved in this oath. They brought their plan to the chief priests and elders and asked them to petition the commander to allow the Sanhedrin to meet again with Paul, under the pretext of seeking more information. These forty men planned to lie in wait for Paul and kill him before he arrived at the Sanhedrin. One can only wonder about the spiritual state of these religious leaders who became involved in such a murderous plot.

What the council did not understand was that the Lord God himself was protecting Paul. By the Lord's providence, Paul's nephew heard about this plot and immediately went to tell Paul about it. Paul asked one of the centurions to take the young boy to the commander. After listening to Paul's nephew, the commander dismissed the young boy, telling him to speak to no one on this matter.

The commander called two centurions and told them to prepare a detachment of two hundred soldiers, seventy horsemen, and two hundred spearmen to leave for Caesarea that night with Paul, taking him directly to Governor Felix. The commander gave the soldiers a letter for Felix which explained that the Jews had been trying to kill Paul when troops had rescued him. The letter also stated that the commander had been unable to discover why the Jews were accusing Paul, and so he had Paul brought before the Sanhedrin. This council, however, had not brought a charge and neither had the commander found anything about Paul that was deserving of death or imprisonment. When the commander had discovered that a plot was to be carried out against Paul, he decided to send him directly to Felix for his judgment.

The soldiers took Paul that night and brought him to Antipatris. The next day they arrived in Caesarea. After presenting Paul and the letter to Felix, the soldiers returned to Jerusalem. Felix placed Paul in prison, awaiting the arrival of his accusers.

We cannot help but be struck here by the way God protected Paul against those who sought his life. God placed a hedge around Paul that the enemy could not penetrate. God had been throwing the enemy into confusion. Paul must have been smiling to himself as he saw his enemy's plans being foiled repeatedly.

What courage we can take in the story of Paul's ordeal. God was not finished with Paul. There was nothing his enemies could do to him. Paul was destined to go to Rome as God had promised. God was completely sovereign in this trial. What is your trial today? God is sovereign over your trial as well. Through the enemies of Paul, God was working out his perfect will. God will do this in your life as well.

For Consideration:

* What does this passage teach us about how God watches over his people?

- In what ways did God show his sovereignty over Paul's enemies in this passage? What courage do you take from this?

For Prayer:

- Ask the Lord to forgive you for the times you have doubted his care for you.

- Thank him that he is watching over you right now in your trial.

39

Paul's Trial

Part 3: His Defense before Felix

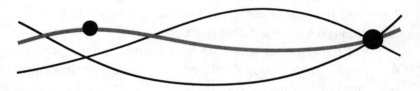

Read Acts 24:1–27

Paul was under guard, awaiting his accusers from Jerusalem. It did not take them long to come. Within five days the high priest Ananias, some elders, and a lawyer named Tertullus arrived in Caesarea where Paul was being held. This delegation came to bring their charges against Paul. Tertullus presented the case to Governor Felix.

Notice how Tertullus began his argument. He took the time to praise Felix for his excellent leadership. He reminded Felix of how, under his leadership, the Jews had enjoyed a period of peace. Tertullus praised and thanked Felix for his many good reforms. These words of Tertullus were pure flattery because Governor Felix was a very brutal and cruel leader.

After falsely praising Felix, Tertullus got to the matter at hand. He accused Paul of being a troublemaker, stirring up riots, being a ringleader of the Nazarene sect (one of the names they called Christians), and desecrating the temple. If these accusations were true and could be proven, Paul would have been in serious trouble. The Jews who had come with Tertullus joined him in support of these accusations.

As was the custom, Paul was then given the opportunity to speak in his own defense. Paul did not stoop to false praise. He was glad to be able to defend himself before Felix, who had been governor for a number of years and who would have had a certain understanding of Jewish ways. Felix also would have seen the tension between the Jews and the Christians. This knowledge would help Felix understand why the Jews were so upset.

Paul told Felix that twelve days before, he had gone to the temple to worship. While he was there, the Jews had not found him arguing with anyone or stirring up the crowd either in the synagogue or in the city. He told Felix that his accusers had no proof for any of the accusations they had brought against him. There was one accusation, however, that Paul would not deny: he was indeed a member of the Way (or as they called him, a Nazarene). Paul would not deny that he was a follower of the Lord Jesus and that he believed what the Old Testament prophets had predicted about the coming Messiah. Paul expressed a hope in the resurrection of both the righteous and the wicked, and so he sought to live with a clean conscience before God and mankind. In this brief statement, Paul told Felix that the Lord Jesus was the Messiah prophesied in the Old Testament Scriptures. He also told Felix that Jesus was coming again to judge the world. Everyone needed to be ready for his return. Paul was unashamed of his hope in Christ. He took advantage of this moment to share with Felix, in a very quiet and unassuming way, his hope in Christ.

From this brief gospel presentation, Paul stated that he had been absent from Jerusalem for twelve years and had returned to bring gifts for the poor (possibly gifts he had received from the churches for the poor in Jerusalem). We read about these gifts in 1 Corinthians 16:1–4. Paul also had come to offer some personal offerings to the Lord. When his accusers had found him presenting his offerings in the temple courts, there had been no crowd with him nor was he causing a disturbance. Paul admitted that a riot in Jerusalem had started because of him. We read about this in Acts 21:27–36. At that time, Jews from Asia saw Paul in the temple and started a false rumor that he had taken Gentiles into the temple. These Asian Jews, however, were not present before Felix that day. Paul reminded those present that he had already been tried on this matter in Jerusalem, and the Sanhedrin had not been able to accuse him of any crime. Believing in the resurrection of the dead was not a crime in Jewish or Roman law.

Having heard Paul's defense, Felix adjourned the proceedings, saying that when Lysias the commander came, he would make his decision. Lysias was the commander who had sent Paul to Caesarea (see Acts 23:12–30). Felix then placed Paul under guard, but his friends were allowed to visit him and care for his needs.

Several days later Felix came with his Jewish wife, Drusilla, to meet with Paul. They listened to Paul speak about his faith in the Lord Jesus. When Paul shared with Felix about righteousness, self-control, and judgment, Felix became afraid. As we have already mentioned, Felix was a cruel and brutal leader. Listening to Paul made him realize that he would one day give an account of his actions before God. Instead of repenting, Felix blocked his ears. He told Paul that he did not want to hear any more and that he would send for him when it was convenient. Although Felix did send for Paul on a regular basis (see verse 26), his motives were very questionable. He hoped to get a bribe from Paul. This shows us that he knew that Paul was innocent. He had nothing against Paul to merit a sentence, but he kept Paul in prison, hoping to get something for himself.

What is important for us to notice here is that Felix, though convicted by the message of Paul, chose to turn his back on it. How many people have found themselves in a similar situation? Maybe as you read this meditation you find yourself in the shoes of Felix. Maybe there are certain things in your life that the Lord has been speaking to you about. He is asking you to make things right, but you are not yet ready. Like Felix, you say that you will listen again when it is more convenient. We have no record of Felix ever taking Paul's message to heart. Maybe at first he truly did want to hear what Paul had to say. When he found out that the message required that he deal with his sin, he refused to listen. Outwardly, it seemed that he was very interested. He continued to call for Paul and to speak often with him. Inwardly, his motives were wrong. He was looking for a bribe. There are many people like this today. They keep coming to church and prayer meetings, but in their hearts, they have chosen to ignore the message. On the inside, sin is eating them up. Maybe that could describe your life.

Paul would remain in prison for two years. Another governor would replace Felix. We may very well wonder about the purpose of this imprisonment. Why did the great apostle Paul need to be kept in prison for two years when he had done nothing wrong? God was working out his purposes in the life of Paul and the early church. Paul discovered that because of his imprisonment, the churches were becoming bolder in their outreach. Listen to what he wrote to the Philippians: "Now I want you to know, brothers, that what has happened to me has really served to advance the gospel. As a result, it has become clear throughout the whole palace guard and to everyone else that I am in chains for Christ. Because of my chains, most of the brothers in the

Lord have been encouraged to speak the word of God more courageously and fearlessly" (Philippians 1:12–14).

Remember that during this time in prison, Paul wrote many of his letters. These letters would form a significant part of the New Testament. Today we are still benefiting from these prison letters. During this time Paul was no longer able to move from one city to another. He was confined to his quarters. His ministry was limited. He had plenty of time to spend with the Lord. I have no doubt that the prayer life of the apostle grew during this time. He had time to listen to what the Lord was saying to him. His ministry, though limited physically, was spiritually powerful. Would Paul have done so much writing were it not for his confinement? In all of these trials, God was working out his purposes. Paul could not have understood the impact his letters would have on the whole world. I don't believe that he understood that you and I would be impacted in our generation because of his confinement in a prison cell. I don't think he understood how many people would come to the Lord by reading the letters he wrote from that cell. What looks like defeat may in fact be wonderful victory. God's ways are not our ways.

The lesson here for us is that God is sovereign in our trials. He works out his purposes through us. You may not understand your pain now, but be assured that God will use it to bring glory to his name. He has your best interest at heart.

For Consideration:

- Has God been speaking to you, as he spoke to Felix, about some issue where you have been disobedient? Seek God's enabling to make this right.

- Have you seen how God has used trials in your life for good? Explain.

For Prayer:

- Ask the Lord to reveal any sin that he wants you to deal with today.

- Thank him for a particular trial he used in your life to draw you closer to himself.

- Ask him to help you to trust him in the trials that you are facing right now. Thank him that he promises to work out these trials for your good.

40

Paul's Trial

Part 4: His Defense before Festus

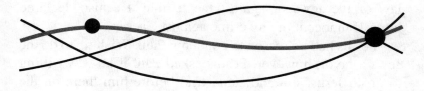

Read Acts 25:1–22

Very soon after taking over the position of Felix as governor of Judea, Festus came to Jerusalem. While he was in Jerusalem, the chief priests and leaders presented him with their case against Paul. Possibly taking advantage of the fact that Festus was new to this position, the Jews strongly urged him to have Paul transferred to Jerusalem. Notice how verse 2 tells us that they urged Festus to do this as a favor to them as Jews. We are left with the idea that there was a certain political motivation behind these words. There was tension between the Jews and the Romans at the best of times. If Festus could procure the good favor of the Jews, he would certainly make himself look good in the eyes of his Roman superiors. Notice that the Jews were not at all interested in having Paul tried. Their only desire was for his death. They planned to have an ambush ready for Paul as he arrived in Jerusalem.

Festus did not fall into the trap of the Jewish religious

leaders. He told them that if they wanted to have Paul tried, they should come to Caesarea where he would meet them and call Paul to stand before them. When Festus returned to Caesarea, he convened the court. Paul was brought out to stand before his accusers. The Jews accused him of many serious offenses. The problem, however, was that none of these crimes could be proven.

Once again, Paul was asked to defend himself before his accusers. Paul's defense seems to have been quite simple. He denied having committed any crime either against the law of the Jews or against the temple. He also declared himself innocent of any crime against Caesar.

Festus had no reason to condemn Paul. Wishing to do the Jews a favor, however, Festus asked Paul if he was willing to go to Jerusalem and stand trial before him there on the charges that had been brought against him. After two years of imprisonment, it would have been understandable that Paul seek any means possible to prove his innocence. He knew, however, the hatred and deceit of these Jews. Paul told Festus that he did not refuse to receive the punishment for any crime he had committed. However, he had done nothing against the Jews. They had tried three times to condemn him without success. Paul knew the Jews would stop at nothing short of his death. He chose to be tried by Rome. Paul appealed to Caesar as the final court of appeal.

As a Roman citizen, Paul had the right to appeal to Caesar. The fact that the Jews had chosen to falsely accuse him of some very serious political offenses (see Acts 24:5) worked to Paul's advantage. Only those cases which were judged important enough could be sent to Caesar. Festus could either dismiss all the charges against Paul and set him free or allow Paul to go to Rome to be tried before Caesar. While we know that Paul's case did not merit the attention of Caesar, the serious and false accusations of the Jews forced the hand of Festus. Once again, we see how God sovereignly worked out his purposes in Paul's life. Even the false accusations of the Jews were used by God to bring Paul to Rome.

A few days after the decision of Festus to send Paul to Caesar, King Agrippa and his sister Bernice arrived in Caesarea to pay their respects to the new governor. (Agrippa had been appointed king of the Roman region of Chalcis by Emperor Claudius.) Festus had the opportunity to discuss Paul's case with Agrippa. Festus explained that the accusations ultimately boiled down to a religious dispute about the person of Christ, whom Paul claimed to be alive. Festus told Agrippa how Paul had requested to be sent to Caesar. Agrippa was intrigued by the trial and asked if he could hear Paul. Festus agreed to bring Paul before him the next day.

Despite the fact that the trial of the apostle Paul had been going on for over two years, God was still working in his life. God's timing is not ours. There are times when we get anxious and question the ways of the Lord. It would seem reasonable that even the apostle Paul would have wondered what God was doing in his life. Paul had now been tried in four courts. Now Agrippa wanted to hear his case. Maybe you feel like one obstacle after another is being thrown into your path. God is working out his purposes even as he was for Paul. Submit to God's timing. He will accomplish everything he sets his hand to do. Let him work. He will work it all out in the end.

For Consideration:

• Why is it so hard to wait on the Lord?

• What promises does God give to those who wait on him?

- Are there things in your life for which you presently have to wait? Is there any reason to doubt that the Lord will not do what is right in his own time?

For Prayer:

- Ask the Lord for patience to wait on him and his timing.

- Thank him that he is a sovereign God who has all things in control.

- Do you know people who have faced one obstacle after another in their lives? Ask God to minister to them in their trials.

- Thank the Lord that he will overcome all obstacles in the end.

41

Paul's Trial

Part 5: His Defense before Agrippa

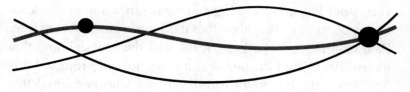

Read Acts 25:23–26:32

This was the fifth time the apostle Paul stood on trial for crimes he had not committed. Paul had been held as a prisoner for over two years, yet he had not been found guilty of any crime. In this fifth defense, Paul would stand before Agrippa. King Agrippa came to the trial with great pomp. He was dressed in his royal robes with his sister Bernice at his side. Also with him came the highest-ranking officers and leading men of the city of Caesarea. If Agrippa was trying to make an impression, he no doubt had succeeded.

When everyone was in place, at the command of Governor Festus, Paul was brought in. Festus told the king how the Jewish communities of Jerusalem and Caesarea had petitioned him to have this man executed. Festus, however, had found in him no crime worthy of death. Because Paul had made an appeal to Caesar, Festus was forced to send him to Rome. The problem was that Festus had no accusation to bring against Paul. Therefore, Festus brought the apostle before Agrippa with the hope that he might be able to find some charge against Paul for Caesar to try.

After the introductory comments of Festus, Agrippa looked to Paul and gave him permission to speak in his own defense. Paul began by telling Agrippa that he felt very privileged to stand before him. Paul knew that Agrippa was well acquainted with the customs and the beliefs of the Jews. Paul proceeded to share with King Agrippa the story of his conversion. Paul told Agrippa how he had grown up as a very strict Jew and had a hope in the resurrection of the dead. It was because of this hope that the Jews were accusing him. Paul claimed that the Lord Jesus was the Messiah and that he had risen from the dead. The Jews not only rejected this but also actively sought to kill anyone who promoted this doctrine.

Paul went on to say that at one point in his life, he was just like these Jews in their opposition to the person of Jesus. On the authority of the chief priests, Paul himself had become a leader in opposition to the spread of Christianity. He had cast many Christians into prison and was also responsible for having many executed for their faith. He had traveled from one synagogue to another, dragging out Christians to punish them for their beliefs. Paul told Agrippa that he had even tried to force Christians to blaspheme the name of the Lord Jesus. Paul spread this persecution of Christians to foreign countries. Paul's testimony to Agrippa shed great light on the intensity of Paul's early hatred of Christians. It did not surprise Paul that the Jews had such a bitter anger against him now. He had experienced this in his own life before coming to Christ.

There is no one in the Bible who speaks more about the grace of God than the apostle Paul. It is not hard to understand why the theme of grace has such an important place in Paul's heart. Could the Lord possibly forgive him for his sins? After all he had done against the work of the Lord, could he ever be accepted before God? The exciting truth is that there is absolute forgiveness in Christ. The blood of the Lord Jesus covered all of Paul's sins. Not one of his crimes would be held against him on the day of judgment. This is nothing short of grace.

Paul continued his testimony by telling Agrippa that on one of his campaigns against the followers of Jesus, he was on his way to Damascus when a bright light from heaven struck him. Both he and his companions fell to the ground. Paul heard a voice speaking to him out of that light. The voice said: "Saul, Saul, why do you persecute me? It is hard for you to kick against the goads" (verse 14). The goad was a long rod with a pointed end used to encourage an ox to go in the right direction. The impression we get here is that God had been working in the life of the apostle long before his conversion. Paul was fighting against God early in his life. The time came for him to stop fighting and submit to the prompting of God's Spirit.

Paul did not really know who was speaking to him in this light. He asked the voice to identify itself. The voice responded: "I am Jesus, whom you are persecuting" (verse 15). Jesus then told Paul to get up on his feet. He told Paul that he had a purpose for his life: to be his witness. Paul would be Christ's ambassador to bring light to the Gentiles. Through his ministry many would be delivered from the power of the devil and receive forgiveness of sins through the Lord Jesus. This would not be an easy task. Paul would be persecuted by both the Gentiles and the Jews. The Lord Jesus promised him, however, that he would protect him from his enemies.

Paul turned his attention to King Agrippa: "King Agrippa, I was not disobedient to the vision from heaven" (verse 19). Paul told Agrippa how from that time onward he set his heart to share the message of repentance and forgiveness through the Lord Jesus. It was because of this message that the Jews hated him. They wanted to kill him because of his faith in the Lord Jesus. God had protected him, however, just as he had promised. His message was not contrary to the teachings of the Jewish Scriptures. In fact, the Scriptures themselves taught that the Messiah would suffer, die, and be raised from the dead. They also taught that this Messiah would proclaim light to both the Jews and the Gentiles.

It was at this point that Festus interjected. He told Paul that he was a fool. It is not clear why Festus felt this way. Was it because of Paul's story about a light from heaven? Was it the way in which Paul risked his life to present the message of salvation? Was it simply an overall rejection of the Jewish and Christian faith? We are not told.

Paul had greater hopes for King Agrippa. While the heart of Festus was steeped in his Roman religion, Agrippa had an appreciation for the Jewish faith. Paul knew that Agrippa was more familiar with the Jewish faith than Festus. Paul knew that Agrippa believed in the prophets and had heard about the ministry of Jesus. There was a gentle pleading in Paul's words. Paul pleaded with Agrippa to accept the clear teaching of the prophets he claimed to believe. Like Festus, however, Agrippa was not ready to accept Paul's message. "Do you think that in such a short time you can persuade me to be a Christian?" was his reply to Paul (verse 28). It seems that Agrippa understood the desire of Paul to see him accept the Lord Jesus. Paul unashamedly told Agrippa that it was his desire that not only the king but everyone present for this trial would come to accept the Lord Jesus, even as he had. Even though Paul was the one in chains, he knew a freedom that no one else in that room knew. We again catch a glimpse of the heart of Paul for the lost.

When Paul finished speaking, Agrippa rose to his feet and left with all who had come to listen to Paul's defense. As he left he said: "This man is not doing anything that deserves death or imprisonment. . . . This man could have been set free if he had not appealed to Caesar" (verses 31–32).

Paul had received his commission from the Lord on the road to Damascus. As he shared his testimony, he did so unashamedly. Paul had given his all to the work of the Lord. God had called him, and he had obeyed. This was his testimony. As Paul looked back over his life, he knew he had run a good race. He stood on trial unashamed. The day is coming when we will all stand before the Lord to give an account of our lives and ministries. Will we be able to look back on our lives and be unashamed like Paul?

For Consideration:

- Notice how Paul always felt compelled to be obedient to his calling. What do you suppose kept this vision alive?

- What things tend to diminish our sense of God's calling in our lives?

- Are there things in your life that bring you shame? What does this passage tell you about the forgiveness of God?

- Notice how freely Paul shared his faith in Christ. Do you have this same freedom?

For Prayer:

- Praise the Lord for the boldness of Paul. Ask the Lord to give you some of this boldness.

- Thank the Lord for his forgiveness. If there are things for which you need forgiveness, ask the Lord to forgive you right now.

- Pray for your spiritual leaders. Ask the Lord to help them keep their spiritual calling fresh.

42

Voyage to Rome

Read Acts 27:1–44

After over two years of waiting, the day arrived when it was determined that the apostle Paul would go to Rome. Paul and several other prisoners were handed over to a centurion named Julius. They boarded a ship from Adramyttium that was headed for ports along the coast of Asia. In verse 2 we read that Aristarchus was with Paul as he sailed. According to Acts 19:29, Aristarchus was one of Paul's traveling companions on his third missionary journey. This meant that the Lord had provided Paul with at least one Christian companion for the journey. The use of the words "we" and "us" indicates that there might have been other believers traveling with Paul on this journey.

The first day's journey took them to the port of Sidon, approximately eighty miles (one hundred and thirty kilometers) from Caesarea. There Julius allowed Paul to spend time with some friends, who provided for his basic needs for the voyage. We should remember that in those days, prisoners were not cared for in the way they are today in some countries. God was with Paul in this journey and had given him favor with the centurion. God was also providing for Paul's needs through the believers along the way.

From Sidon Paul's group set out to sea again. This time they sailed past the island of Cyprus, Paul's first stop on his first missionary journey. No doubt, Paul thought about the believers on this island as he sailed past. The sailing party landed at the port of Myra some three hundred and fifty miles (five hundred and seventy kilometers) west of Sidon. There they boarded another ship headed for Italy.

Progress toward Italy was very slow because of high winds. With difficulty they arrived off Cnidus (a distance of approximately one hundred and fifty miles or two hundred and forty kilometers). Because of the winds, the sailors were forced to veer from their course to the south, finally arriving at the port of Fair Havens some one hundred and ninety miles or three hundred kilometers southwest of Cnidus. The winds had caused much loss of time. It was now getting late in the season and sailing would become more and more dangerous.

Paul understood that if they continued their journey, it would end in disaster. He warned those on board that there would be loss of the ship, its cargo, and possibly loss of lives if they continued. Considering that the port at Fair Havens was not suitable to winter the ship, however, the centurion chose to listen to the pilot and continue sailing to the port of Phoenix, less than sixty miles (one hundred kilometers) away. The pilot convinced the centurion that they could reach this port without difficulty and it promised to be a much better location to winter the ship.

When the winds changed, Paul's group set out for Phoenix. They were hardly out to sea when a hurricane struck and the ship was driven out into the open sea. A journey the sailors thought would only take a few hours ended up being a fourteen-day nightmare in the open sea. Does this not teach us a very valuable lesson? Paul had a word from the Lord and advised the sailors that they were better to stay in the region of Fair Havens. But the centurion and the pilot felt that they knew better. They refused the word of the Lord and set out in their own wisdom. How many of us are like that? How many times have we ended up on the open sea because we have chosen to ignore the Word of God? Like the pilot and the centurion, we may think that we are close to achieving some goal. We can handle it. When we set out, however, the winds of sin engulf us and sweep us off course.

In the storm the ship almost lost its lifeboat off the coast of Cauda. Then fearful that the whole ship would be torn apart, the sailors secured ropes under it in a feeble attempt to keep it together. At another point there was fear of running aground, so the crew cast the anchor overboard in the hope that it would catch on the bottom and keep the ship from running into the sandbars. There was no choice but to let the ship go with the wind. On the third day in an attempt to lighten the ship, the crew threw the cargo and tackle overboard. All hopes of making any profit on this journey were gone. The only desire of those on the ship was to live through this horrible experience. In the days that followed, they saw no sign of sun or stars. Because this was the only way that these sailors could know their location, they were lost at sea and resigned to the fact that they were all going to die. Days passed without anyone eating food.

It was into this situation of despair that an angel of the Lord appeared to Paul and told him that he would stand trial before Caesar. God was going to save the lives of every individual on board the ship. Paul told them all to take courage because he had confidence that everything would happen just as the angel had predicted.

After fourteen days at sea, the sailors sensed that they were heading toward land. When they took soundings, they discovered that this was the case. Their greatest fear was that they would be dashed against the rocks and thrown into the violence of the waves. The crew dropped four anchors and prayed for safety.

Realizing the seriousness of the situation, the sailors attempted to abandon the ship. They lowered the lifeboat in an attempt to escape. Paul told the soldiers, however, that unless these men stayed with the ship, they would die. The soldiers cut the ropes to the lifeboat and let it fall into the sea. Paul then encouraged everyone to eat and reminded them of the promise of God that all of them would be safe. Paul led them in a prayer of thanksgiving for the food and they all ate. This seemed to revive their spirits. When everyone had finished eating, they cast the remainder of the grain overboard to lighten the ship. There were 276 individuals on board the ship.

When daylight came, the sailors sighted land and a sandy bay. They decided to run the ship aground into this bay. To do this the anchors were cut loose, the ropes that held the rudders were untied, and the foresail was hoisted to the wind. This drove the ship with full force toward the beach. When the ship struck a sandbar, however, the bow stuck fast and stern was shattered by the waves.

At this point the soldiers planned to kill the prisoners because they feared the punishment of death if any escaped. Paul had made such a deep impression on the centurion, however, that he wanted to spare Paul's life and kept the soldiers from carrying out their plan. Instead, the centurion ordered that any who could swim jump overboard and head for the beach. Those who could not swim were to cling to the planks and boards that had been broken off the ship. In this way everyone reached the shore safely, just as Paul had said.

We have seen how the centurion and the pilot ignored the word of the Lord through Paul at Fair Havens. Because of this the ship had been forced into the open sea and its terrors. There are many today, like these sailors, who have ignored the Word of God and are adrift on the open sea, experiencing the horror of sin. What is important for us to notice here, however, is that this is not the end of the story. The horror was real. The crew lost the cargo and all hope of profit from this voyage. God had not forsaken them, however. There was still hope in him. It was not too late.

The sailors were guilty of ignoring wise warning. The shape and direction of their lives had radically changed, but by God's grace none of them lost their lives. Through Paul, God offered them hope. God is doing the same for us today. He offers us hope right now. There is still forgiveness even when we have really messed up and disobeyed him. The sailors almost missed out on that hope when they attempted for the second time to take matters into their own hands and escape in the lifeboat. Don't be like those sailors. Let God have his way. Only in obedience is there victory.

For Consideration:

- What do you suppose would have happened if the pilot and the centurion had listened to Paul in the first place? How would things have been different?

- Does God give us freedom to make bad choices? What happens when we do? Can God still use these bad decisions to accomplish our good and his glory?

- Has the direction and shape of your life been changed by the bad decisions you have made? How has God used this in your life?

For Prayer:

- Thank the Lord that he did not abandon you in your sin and rebellion.

- Thank the Lord that he is willing to come to our aid although we do not deserve his help.

- Ask God to help you to pay close attention to his Word, so you do not fall into the error of the sailors of this chapter.

- Do you know someone living in rebellion today? Take time to pray for that person.

43

Malta and Rome

Read Acts 28:1–31

Once Paul and all the prisoners were on shore, they found out that they were on the island of Malta. Malta was approximately five hundred and sixty miles (nine hundred kilometers) from Fair Havens, where they had started out fourteen days before. Malta was located just south of Italy. In reality, they were not that far off course. In the fierce storm the Lord had been directing their ship toward Rome.

God's grace is seen also in the way the islanders treated Paul's shipwrecked party. The islander built a fire and welcomed them. As Paul was piling wood on the fire, a viper was driven out by the heat and fastened to his hand. The islanders recognized the snake as venomous. Being superstitious, they believed Paul was deserving of this judgment of the gods because he was a murderer. Paul, however, shook the serpent off his hand into the fire and suffered no ill effects. When the islanders saw this, they were astonished and quickly changed their minds. Instead of seeing Paul as a criminal, they saw him as a god. In reality, we know that this was the hand of God protecting Paul from harm. This object lesson served to show the islanders the power of Paul's God and prepare them to hear the message of salvation through Paul. They would not have listened to a man they considered to be a common criminal. They would listen, however, to one they thought to be a god.

It is quite possible that this incident served to open the door for Paul to see the chief official of the island, a man named Publius, who welcomed them into his home and offered them hospitality. When Paul discovered that the father of Publius was sick in bed with fever and dysentery, he went to see him. When Paul placed his hands on Publius's father, he was healed of his sickness. Realizing what had happened at the hands of Paul, individuals began to come from all parts of the island to be healed of their sicknesses. The islanders in return honored the prisoners and soldiers in many ways, even providing them with all the provisions necessary for the continued journey to Rome.

We can only wonder what the soldiers and prisoners were thinking as they saw the hand of God at work in the life of the apostle Paul. They could not brush these events off lightly. We do not know if any came to accept the Lord Jesus, but we do know that their acquaintance with the apostle must have had a profound impact on their lives.

Paul's party stayed on Malta for three months. After this time, the centurion boarded all his prisoners on a ship and sailed to Syracuse, about ninety miles (one hundred and fifty kilometers) to the northeast. From Syracuse they sailed about eighty miles (one hundred and twenty kilometers) to the north to the city of Rhegium. The next day, because of favorable winds, they continued on to the city of Puteoli, some two hundred miles (three hundred and thirty kilometers) northwest of Rhegium. Puteoli was approximately one hundred miles (one hundred and seventy kilometers) south of the city of Rome. Paul spent a week in Puteoli with some Christians in the city. Believers from that area who had heard that Paul was arriving came to meet with the apostle. Verse 15 tells us that it was a real encouragement to Paul to see these believers coming out to meet him.

Paul was brought to Rome from Puteoli. In Rome Paul was granted the privilege of living by himself with a guard assigned to him. Paul was also given freedom to preach. Only three days after his arrival, Paul called a meeting of the leaders of the Jews. He told them that though he had done nothing wrong, he had been handed over to the Roman authorities. The Romans had examined him and found no crime in him. They would have released him but the Jews had objected. He had appealed to Caesar and was now awaiting his trial.

The Jews of Rome had not heard anything about this matter. They were very curious, however, to hear what Paul believed because they had heard much about these followers of Jesus. A meeting was arranged. A large crowd came to the place where Paul was staying. From morning until evening, Paul spoke to them about the matters of the kingdom of God. He sought to convince them about the Lord Jesus by means of the Law of Moses and the Prophets. Some came to faith in the Lord Jesus because of these discussions. Others refused to believe. What was particularly difficult for the Jews of Rome was when Paul quoted from Isaiah 6:9–10. In this passage God told Isaiah to go to a people who would not listen to his words, a people whose hearts were hardened and whose eyes and ears were closed. The Jews knew that Paul was referring to them as he quoted this passage. When Paul told them that God was offering his salvation to the Gentiles, this was too much for the Jews to handle and many of them left.

For two years Paul stayed in Rome in a rented house

and preached the gospel to all who came to see him. He was unhindered in his proclamation of the gospel during these two years. The fact that he was a prisoner of Rome may well have been an added security for Paul. Rome itself had given Paul freedom to preach the gospel. There was nothing his enemies could do to him.

It is impossible to read the story of Paul's arrest and trials without seeing the hand of a sovereign God working out his purposes. Repeatedly, Paul was protected through his sufferings. God's hand of security and grace was on Paul's life. God did not forsake him in his struggles but worked through the trials he placed in Paul's life to accomplish his glory. God will do the same in your life. While Paul's life was filled with difficulties, God's grace was greater than any trial Paul had to endure. As long as God had a ministry for Paul, his enemies could not hinder him. Paul did not fear the obstacles that came his way. He courageously faced them and let God accomplish his purposes through them. We need to follow Paul's example today. It was in the midst of the obstacles that the power of God was most evident in the life of Paul. May God give us the grace necessary to face our struggles as did the apostle Paul. Like him, we too will find that God's grace is sufficient for every trial.

For Consideration:

- While shipwrecked, Paul performed many miracles. How did those miracles help in the proclamation of the gospel to the islanders?

- How did God use Paul's chains for the furtherance of the gospel?

- How has God used your struggles to advance the gospel?

For Prayer:

- What trials are you facing right now? Ask the Lord to use them to glorify his name.

- Thank God for the lessons he has taught you in your trials.

- Ask the Lord to give you the patience you need to wait on him and trust him in those trials.

Light To My Path
Devotional Commentary Series

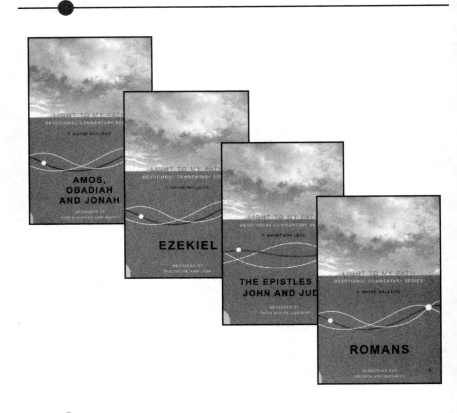

Now Available

Old Testament

- Ezra, Nehemiah, and Esther
- Ezekiel
- Amos, Obadiah, and Jonah
- Micah, Nahum, Habakkuk, and Zephaniah

New Testament

- John
- Acts
- Romans
- The Epistles of John and Jude

A new commentary series
for every day devotional use.

───────────────────────────●──────

"I am impressed by what I have read from this set of commentaries. I have found them to be concise, insightful, inspiring, practical and, above all, true to Scripture. Many will find them to be excellent resources."

Randy Alcorn
director of Eternal Perspective Ministries,
Author of *The Grace & Truth Paradox*
and *Money, Possessions & Eternity*

───────────────────────────●──────

Watch for more in the series
Spring 2005

Old Testament
- Israel
- Haggai, Zachariah and Malachi

New Testament
- Philippians and Colossians
- James and 1&2 Peter

Power of Generosity
How to Transform Yourself and Your World

David Toycen

An intimate journey down the road of giving, *The Power of Generosity* will strike a chord with all who want to fulfill a vital part of their humanity–the need to give.

Dave Toycen, President and CEO of World Vision Canada, believes generosity can save lives—both the benefactor's and the recipient's. The act of giving without an ulterior motive inherently nurtures a need human's have for significance. During three decades of traveling to the poorest and most desperate countries, Dave has seen and met individuals who have been freed by acts of generosity.

What is generosity? What motivates a person toward benevolence? *The Power of Generosity* is a practical guide to developing a spirit of generosity, providing thoughtful answers and encouragement for all those looking for ways to be more giving in their lives.

1-932805-10-9   192 Pages

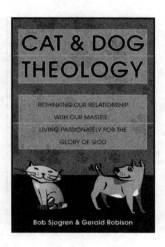

Cat and Dog Theology
Rethinking Our Relationship With Our Master

Bob Sjogren & Dr. Gerald Robison

There is a joke about cats and dogs that conveys their differences perfectly.

> A dog says, "You pet me, you feed me, you shelter me, you love me, you must be God."
> A cat says, "You pet me, you feed me, you shelter me, you love me, I must be God."

These God-given traits of cats ("You exist to serve me") and dogs ("I exist to serve you") are often similar to the theological attitudes we have in our view of God and our relationship to Him. Using the differences between cats and dogs in a light-handed manner, the authors compel us to challenge our thinking in deep and profound ways. As you are drawn toward God and the desire to reflect His glory in your life, you will worship, view missions, and pray in a whole new way. This life-changing book will give you a new perspective and vision for God as you delight in the God who delights in you.

1-884543-17-0   206 Pages

An Introduction To The New Testament
Three Volume Collection

D. Edmond Hiebert

Though not a commentary, the Introduction to the New Testament presents each book's message along with a discussion of such questions as authorship, composition, historical circumstances of their writing, issues of criticism and provides helpful, general information on their content and nature. The bibliographies and annotated book list are extremely helpful for pastors, teachers, and laymen as an excellent invitation to further careful exploration.

This book will be prized by all who have a desire to delve deeply into the New Testament writings.

1-884543-74-X   976 Pages